Pop-Up Paper Spheres
23 Beautiful Projects to Make with Paper and Scissors

Seiji Tsukimoto

SCHIFFER
PUBLISHING

4880 Lower Valley Road • Atglen, PA 19310

Preface

I have been fond of making crafts since childhood. When I found a toy or craft item that I liked, I tried to recreate the item or toy instead of asking my parents to buy it for me. I cherished all of the items that I made. I still remember how much fun it was to view my completed projects all lined up in front of me.

When I encountered pop-up picture books for the first time, I was very impressed. It made me want to create my own original pop-up picture books and display them the way I used to display my handcrafted toys. As the first step toward that goal, I began creating pop-up designs.

When assembling my pop-up designs, I tried to use adhesives as little as possible because I strongly believe that paper art creations constructed without adhesive are inherently more beautiful. I attempted to attach my pop-up designs to cards without using adhesives as well, but the finished results often failed to satisfy my expectations. I came to the conclusion that I needed to create pop-up cards where the pop-up design itself doesn't mount to the card. That is where I came up with the idea of the spherical design, my "Spheres."

The spherical pop-up is a novel form of paper art that transforms a flat plane to a sphere with only the slightest force. Constructing my spherical pop-ups doesn't require any innovative techniques. Rather, spherical pop-ups can be created using basic techniques that any pop-up picture book and card employ, without using any binding or printing, and avoiding adhesives and thread. I created my spheres using only materials that I am fond of and removing any elements that don't serve my artistic visions. Aesthetically eye-pleasing, all the works possess a novel allure that is different from pop-up picture books and rectangular pop-up cards.

Constructing a spherical pop-up design may be challenging. However, I believe that you will feel a great amount of satisfaction and joy upon completion of your chosen project. I designed small spherical pop-up cards, which I normally don't do, especially for this book. Please begin with the projects that are the easiest to construct, and experience the joy of creating your own spheres and discovering just how amusing they can be.

I will be extremely pleased if you find some measure of joy in the sphere designs here.

Seiji Tsukimoto

About Pop-Up Sphere

This book presents four different sized cards.

First, the "small" design is the tiniest and has the simplest structure.

Next, there are two types of "medium." They are slightly larger than the "small" sphere. Medium-1 clearly shows motifs inside the sphere when the card is facing forward. Medium-2 has narrower rings and the motifs face forward. That being said, some motifs are added at an angle so you can enjoy viewing the motifs from different angles. Finally, the "large" is obviously the largest. The "large" requires more rings to construct and thus appeals to one's sense of wonder at how enjoyable spherical shapes can be.

The "large" is also the most complicated sphere to construct. With that in mind, I recommend that you make some small and medium spheres prior to making your first large sphere.

The motifs inside your spherical pop-up can be substituted with motifs of your choice. As long as you use the same number of required rings, you'll be able to construct any sphere you choose. Feel free to design your own original motifs and explore all aspects of spherical pop-up creation.

CONTENTS

Small ⋯⋯ 6

Medium ❶ ⋯⋯ 20

Medium ② 30

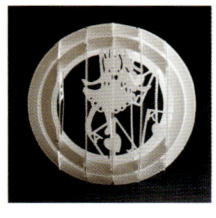

Large 46

Small

This section introduces the small-sized, simplest to construct sphere. This type of sphere is composed of six 7cm (2¾") diameter rings and has a single motif at the center. Create as many as you wish and display them in rows or make a mobile or sculpture to accentuate their petite cuteness. Regular weight drawing paper is durable enough to construct small spheres. Go ahead–start making as many as you wish right now!

Instructions: see p. 18

Patterns: p. 66, 67

8

Messages

Let's cut out letters to send messages. There are two ways to do it: by cutting out the actual letter or by removing material to leave the shape of a letter. This project is a great example of how your font choices can impact the message.

Patterns: p. 66, 68

Cherry Blossom

A single cherry blossom is the motif for this card. Cherry blossoms are quite easy to recognize and are generally symbolic of spring. This card is perfect to send in springtime, but just as lovely all year round.

Patterns: p. 66, 69, 97, 98

Rose

Capture the rose by its outline, just like an artist would in making a stained glass rose. The round shape of the sphere represents the symbolic perfection of a rose.

Patterns: p.66, 69

Here the card is flattened. The overlapped rings create a symmetric, interesting look.

At an angle we see how the rings actually work and the three-dimensional aspect of the sphere is revealed.

Viewing the sphere from the top clearly shows that six rings make up the shape.

Wiggle the flattened card forward and backward while gently pushing both ends to guarantee a spherical shape.

A snowflake is a delicate and picturesque motif. Making small slits and piercing small holes is enough to replicate the intricacies of a snowflake.

Patterns: p.66, 69

A star twinkling on top of a Christmas tree is an easy to make card because a snow-covered tree is such a simple motif.

Patterns: p. 66, 69

All three stars are arranged evenly. Both cards employ basically the same design, but the choice of outlined or cut-out stars alters the overall look.

Patterns: p.66, 69

Crown

Bird

A crown is actually a simple motif, but make sure to completely cut out the design as there are quite a few fine, curved lines.

Patterns: p. 66, 70, 99, 100

Rings encase the bird motif as if it were a birdcage. This card presents an amusing look that only a sphere can deliver. It makes a fantastic ornament in any spot you choose.

Patterns: p. 66, 70

Four-leaf Clover

Hearts

The four-leaf clover is said to bring good luck. Send this card to someone special to wish them the best of luck.

Patterns: p. 66, 70

This is a simple card that combines one big heart and a few small hearts. It makes the perfect Valentine's Day card.

Patterns: p. 66, 70

Use colored paper to create a look that pops.

Connect spheres with
a string to create a mobile.

Instructions: Small

This is the easiest and simplest type of sphere to construct. Making this enables you to understand the basic structure of a sphere. It is recommended that you begin by constructing this type of sphere before moving on.

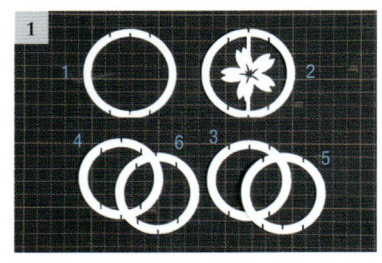

Requires six rings. Join three rings, vertically and horizontally, like a grid. Ring-1 and ring-2 are crossed to make the center of the grid. Rings 3 through 6 are joined to the sides of ring-1 and ring-2.

Join ring-1 and ring-2 by aligning each ring's notches.

Seen from the top, ring-1 and ring-2 are crossed.

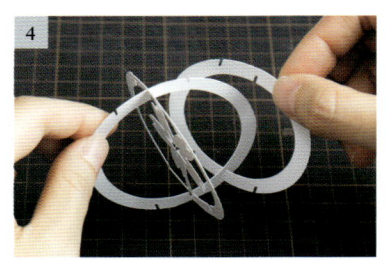

Next, join ring-3. Begin by attaching either the top or bottom notch. The order doesn't matter.

Attach ring-3 parallel to ring-2.

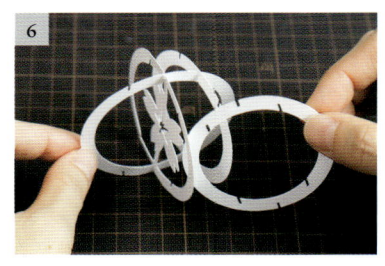

Then, join ring-4 perpendicular to ring-2. Begin assembling the center of the grid and then add the ring that encases the crossed rings.

Join the middle notches of ring-4 with ring-2.

Then, join the side notches with neighboring ring-3. Two vertical and two horizontal rings are joined.

Next, join ring-5 parallel to ring-2. Use the same order.

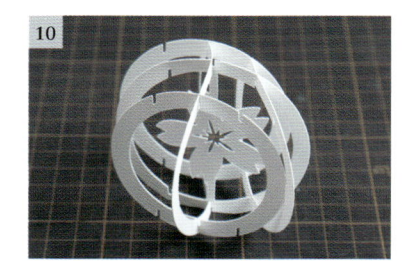

The middle notches are joined.

Be sure to thoroughly connect the notches.

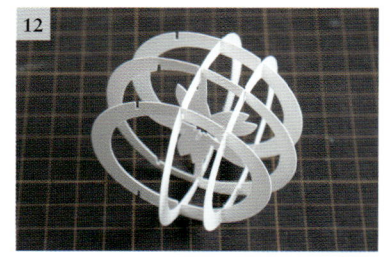

All the horizontal rings are joined. One ring is left.

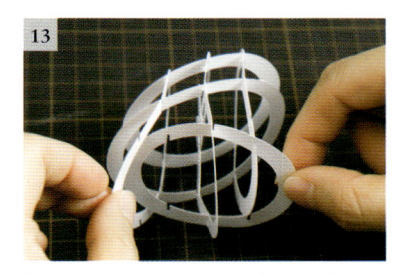

Finally, attach ring-6. First, join the middle notches. Then, the sides.

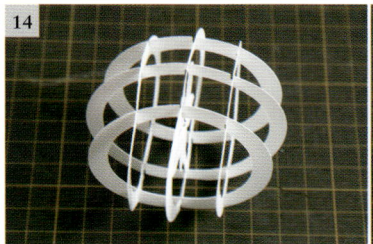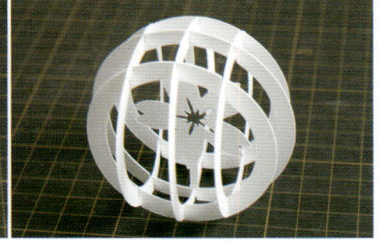

All the rings are now joined in a gridlike manner.

Fold the rings down and iron. Ironing on high for a few seconds will make the paper crisp.

Complete.

Both the small and medium sized spheres begin by joining the rings that make the center of the grid, and then moving outward. Once the center of the grid is connected, there is no specific rule for joining the horizontal or vertical rings. Just remember to alternate directions, vertical and horizontal, when joining each ring to make the grid. If you make a mistake, simply restart the joining process. Rings can be easily removed because they are joined with nothing more than notches.

Sphere

Medium ①

This section introduces the medium-1 sized sphere. The ring diameter is 8 cm / 3⅛" so it is only 1 cm / ⅜" larger than the small sphere. However, the medium-1 size has more rings and a more complex structure; it is composed within a total of nine rings. The motif at the center of the sphere is made out of three of the nine rings. Layering three rings to make the motif creates a certain depth. Since the rings are joined diagonally, the motif at the center is clearly visible from the front-facing view.

Instructions: see p. 28

Happy Birthday

Birthday spheres make perfect greeting cards. Use a sharp object like an awl or needle to pierce holes. These will represent the strawberries' seeds.

Patterns: p. 71, 72

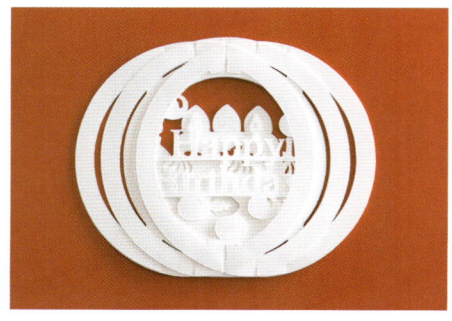

The motif is clearly displayed, even when the sphere is folded flat.

Present

This design for a versatile greeting card combines a gift box and birds. This type of sphere is perfect for a variety of celebratory occasions.

Patterns: p. 71 ~ 73

A simple design like this clearly displays the shape and depth of each motif in the way that only a spherical card can create.

Halloween

This is a fun piece to decorate any room in the house. The motif of ghosts and pumpkins can be projected onto a wall by lighting the sphere with a candle or other light.

Patterns: p. 71, 72, 74

At a certain angle, the ghost at the rear will emerge.

Merry Christmas

This is an intricately designed Christmas card. It is not necessary to outline all the snowflakes and needles inside the tree; instead just make some slits. Cutting slits is enough to add complexity to the motif and produce a realistic look.

Patterns: p. 71, 72, 75, 101~104

Some snowflakes are hidden at the rear. The spherical shape allows for the enjoyment of the card from any angle.

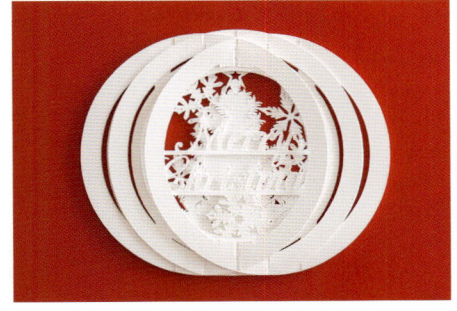

Lily of the Valley and Fairy

This fairy-tale type design
appears as though it were
discovered just peeking out
from a field of flowers. Use
delicate and bold lines to create
the nuanced hair and wings.

Patterns: p. 71, 72, 76

The flowers hidden behind the ring appear by changing an angle.

Assemble the rings diagonally while the motifs are facing forward.

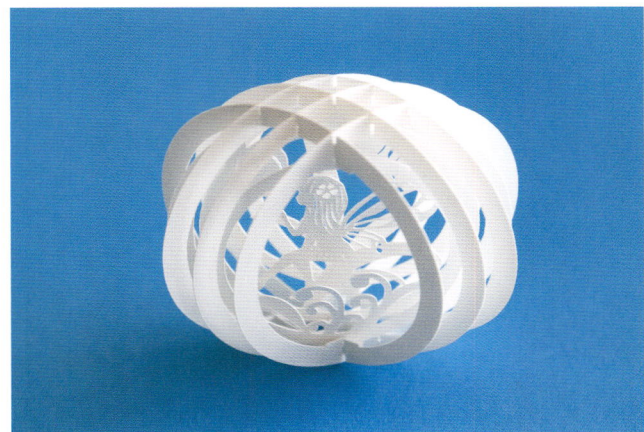

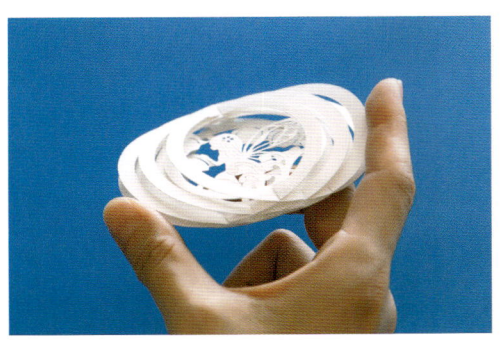

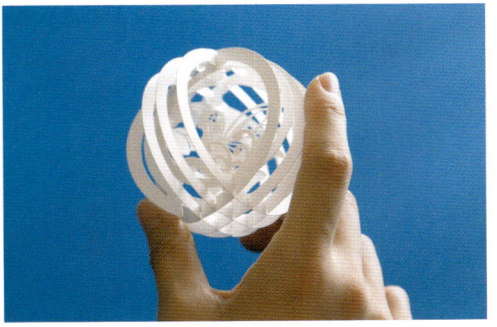

Each neighboring ring fits on top of the other when the sphere is folded down. Push the rings from the sides, thus offsetting the overlapped rings to create a spherical shape.

Instructions: Medium **1**

The medium size sphere requires more rings than the small, but assembling it is still quite simple. From the front, the motif is located between the diagonally crossing rings.

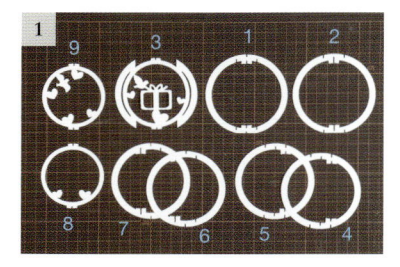

Requires nine rings. Three for the motif are inserted between the diagonals. Rings-1 and -2 are crossed to make the center of the grid. Rings-4, -5, -6, and -7 are joined next. Rings-3, -8, and -9 compose the motif at the center.

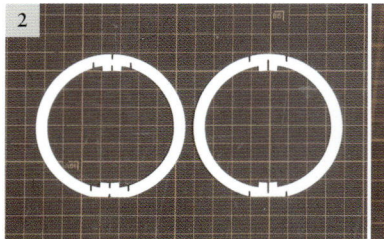

Join rings-1 and -2 while aligning each ring's notches.

Next, join ring-3. It has the motif. This puts the motif at the center.

Insert ring-3 between ring-1 and ring-2 and firmly join the notches. This should stabilize the rings.

Join ring-4 parallel to ring-1. Align ring-4. The protruding notch should be facing up.

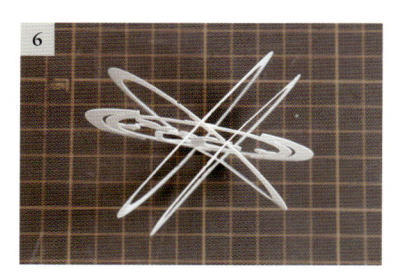

Seen from the top it should look like this.

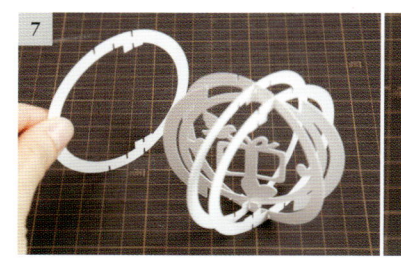

Next, join ring-5 parallel to -1, with the protruding notch facing down. Insert ring-5 across from ring-4.

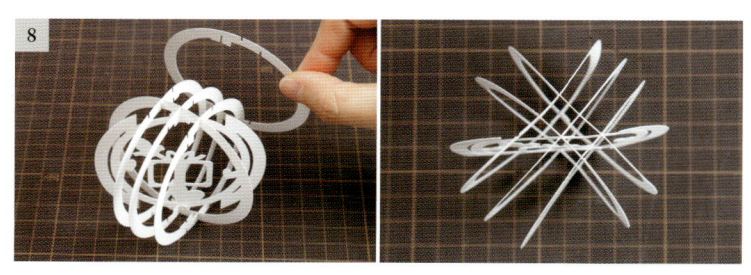

Join ring-6 parallel to ring-2. The protruding notch is facing down.

Across from ring-6, join ring-7. The protruding notch should face up.

Now, all of the rings that make the diagonal grid are joined.

Next, join the motif bearing ring-8. Insert ring-8 where rings-4 and -7 cross.

Seen from top it should look like this. Each motif ring is supported at the top and bottom, thus making the rings movable.

Join ring-9, with the motif, where rings-5 and -6 cross. That is to say, across from ring-8.

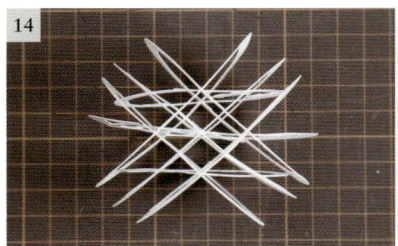
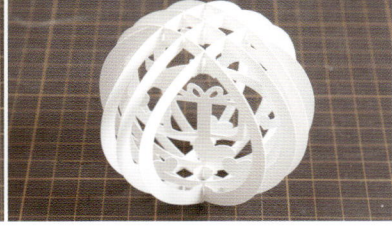

Seen from the top it should look like this. The three rings with the motif are parallel to each other.

Iron on high for a few seconds, same as with the small size, to crisp up the paper.

Complete.

Join the center of the diagonal grid, the center motif, and the outside diagonal grid (the order doesn't matter). Then join the front and rear motif last. The motif rings can be joined inverted. Position as desired.

Medium 2

This section introduces the medium-2 size sphere. Medium-2 uses 7.6 cm / 3" diameter rings that are slightly smaller than medium-1 (presented on p. 20). Medium-2 is composed of eleven rings. Of those, five to seven rings have the motif, which makes this type of sphere more complex. In addition, the width of the rings is narrower than in medium-1. Thus, medium-2 is slightly more challenging than medium-1. The rings with the motifs are inserted at different angles to provide amusing views from any angle.

Instructions: see p. 42

Wedding

The motif — silhouette of a
bride and groom — is perfect
for celebrating a wedding.
A dove, symbol of love and
good fortune, emerges between
the couple.

Patterns: p. 77~79

This card uses many rings. This makes for a more solid spherical shape.

In both the vertical and horizontal directions, the rings joined outside of the center of the grid also have a motif.

Join the rings diagonally for the motifs at the center of sphere. This also creates a slight movement in the motif.

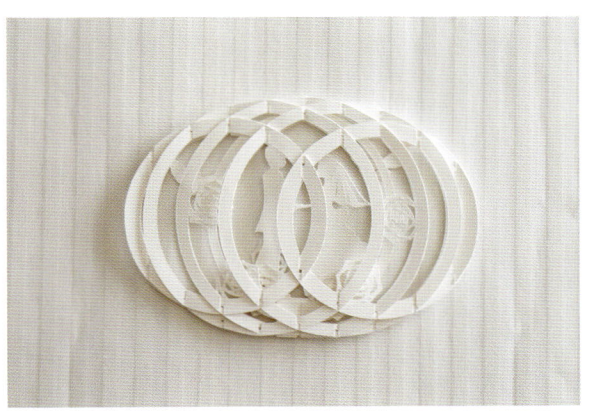

The rings are narrow and delicate.

Alice's Teatime

This design depicts Alice and the White Rabbit at teatime. The motifs are inserted in horizontal and vertical layers, creating a wonderland-like feel.

Patterns: p. 77, 80, 81

Behind Alice is a teapot.

Little Red Riding Hood

This motif shows a girl talking to a wolf. The flower petals surrounding the center motif are narrow. When cutting, pay attention so as not to cut off the petals.

Patterns: p. 77, 82, 83

The flowers are attached both horizontally and vertically.

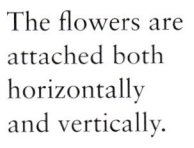

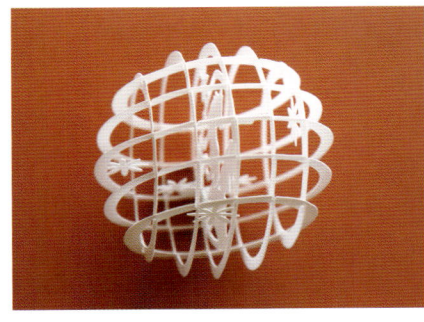

Alice and Cards

This sphere also uses an Alice in Wonderland type image. The numbers and playing card outlines are intricate, so take care not to bend them when joining the rings.

Patterns: p. 77, 84, 85, 105-110

When folded down, this design reveals quite a few playing card motifs.

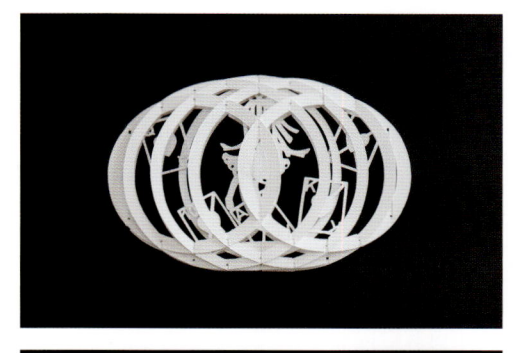

A view from the side.

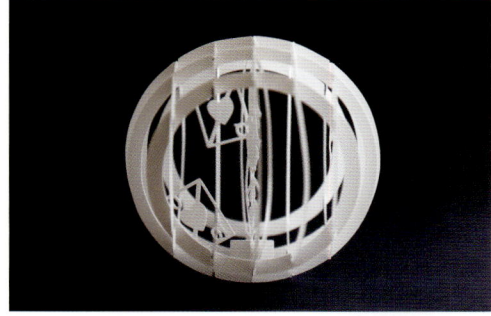

This angle shows how fun spherical shapes can be.

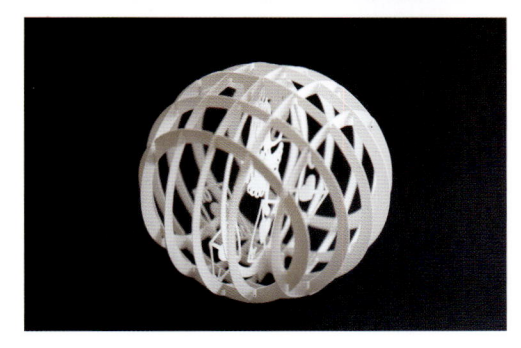

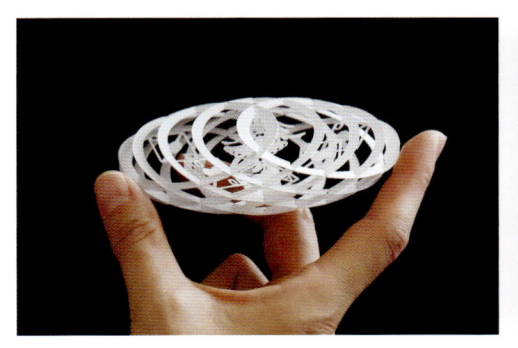 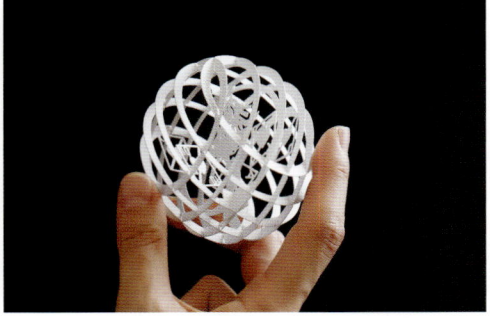

Push both sides to create the spherical shape. Be careful not to bend the rings since they are quite narrow.

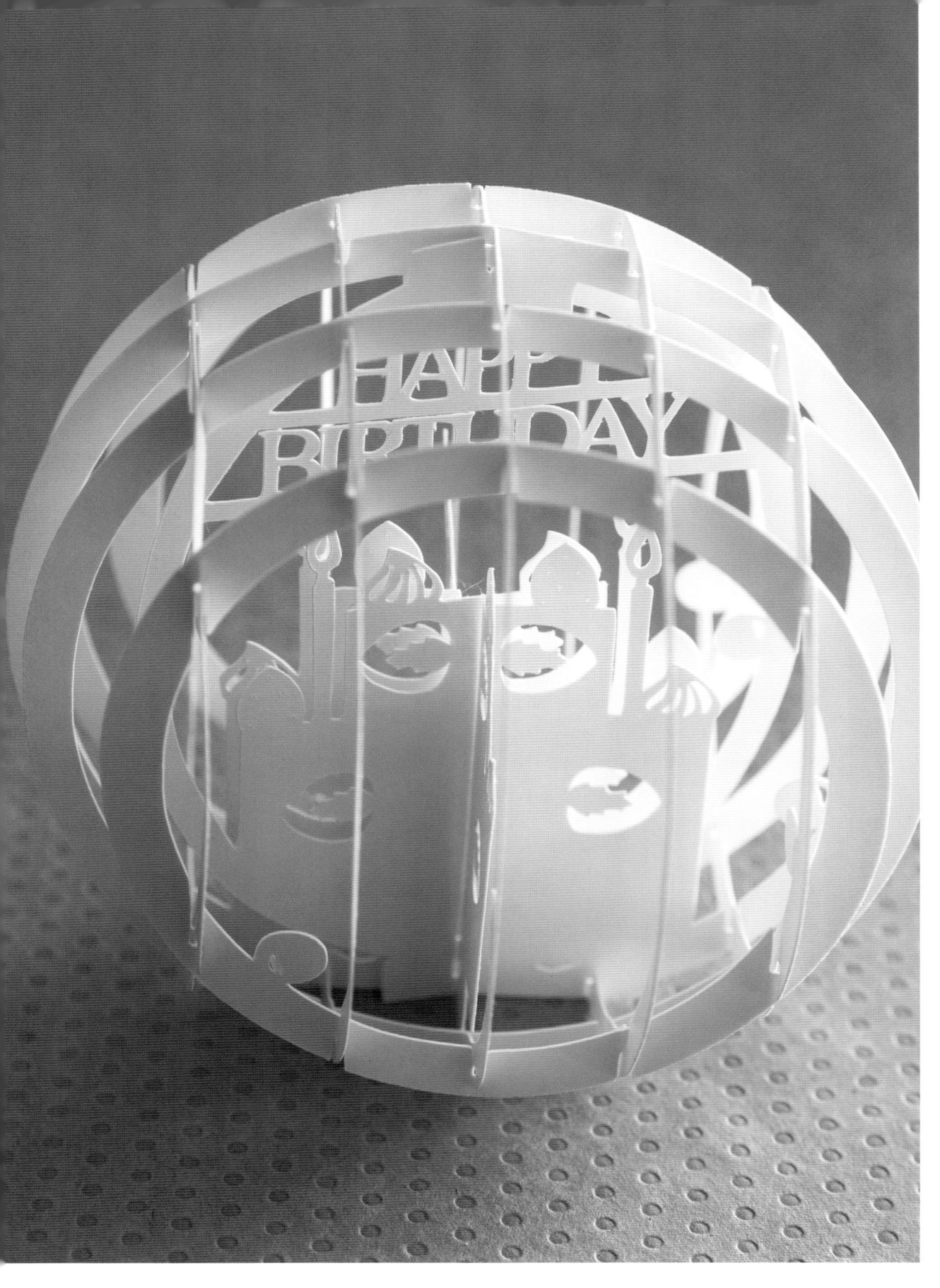

Happy Birthday

This is a birthday card that, from an angle, looks like a three-dimensional birthday cake. The motif is the same as other birthday cards presented in this book, except the number of rings required — and how they are composed — alter the look of the card.

Patterns: p. 77, 86, 87, 111~116

The rings with the cake motif are crossed.

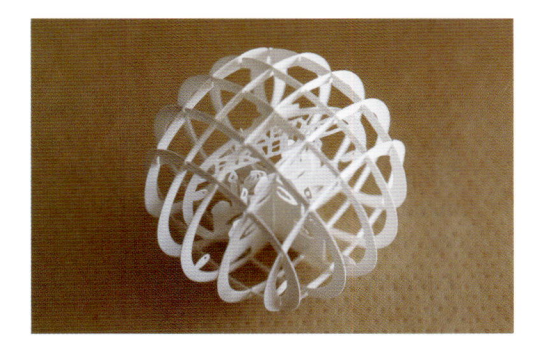

A small ring is joined at the center, where other rings are joined to make a grid.

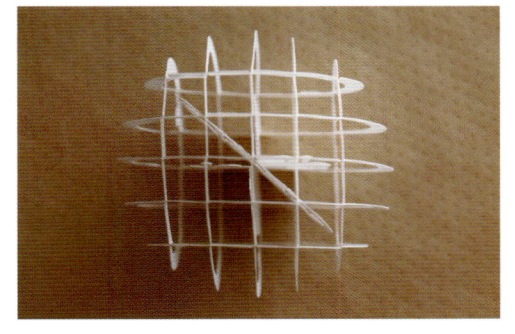

When folded down, the overlapping rings make it look simple.

Three rings have the cake motifs.

Mounting a Sphere on a Card

Mounting a sphere on a card allows for a centerfold-style pop-up. Make the sphere first, then attach it to the card using thread and a needle. The fold-up structure of the sphere allows for a card like this.

Instructions: see p. 44

41

Instructions: Medium ②

This one requires more rings, but the assembling basics are the same as for other sizes. One movable motif is inserted at the center. The rings are narrow and easily bend so be careful.

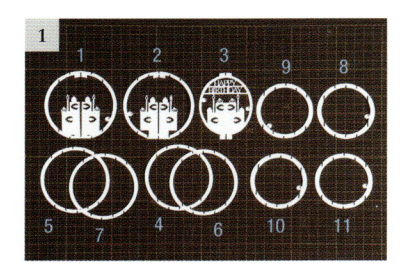

Requires eleven rings. The ring with the motif is inserted at the center of the grid made by five rings joined vertically and horizontally. Rings-1 and -2 are crossed to make the center of the grid. Rings-4 through -11 encase the center. Ring-3 is the motif at the center.

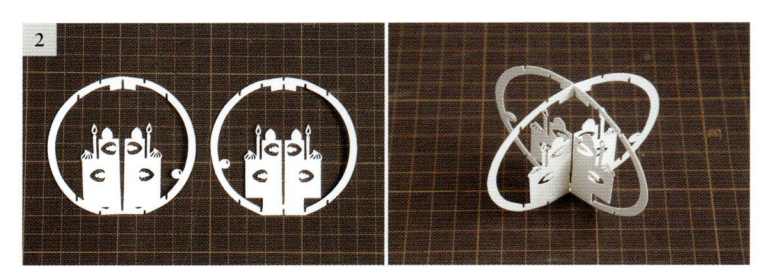

Join rings-1 and -2 aligning each ring's notches.

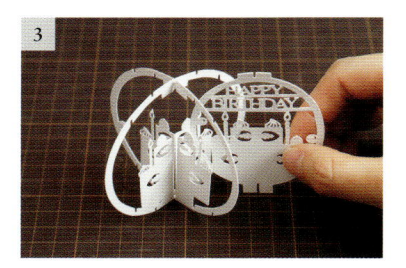

Next, join ring-3, the one with the motifs. These are the motifs at the center.

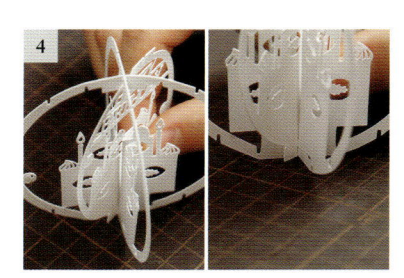

Insert ring-3 between rings-1 and -2 and firmly join the notches. This stabilizes the rings.

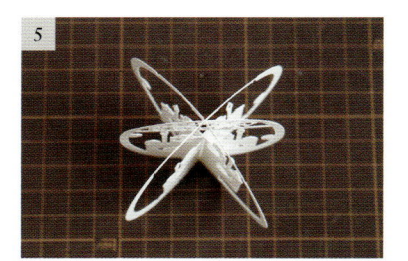

Seen from the top. The motifs are visible from any angle.

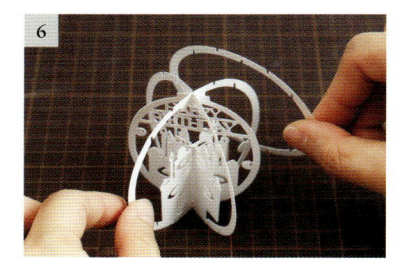

Join ring-4 in parallel behind ring-2.

Firmly join the notches. Be careful not to bend.

Seen from the top.

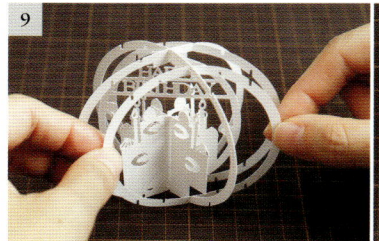

Next, join ring-5 parallel to ring-1, but in front. First, join the top and bottom notches. Then, join the notches with neighboring rings.

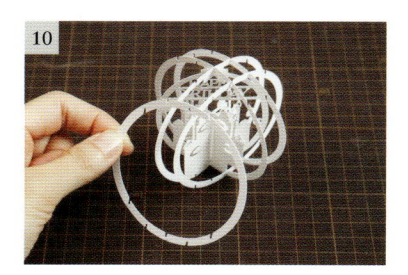

Join ring-6 parallel to ring-2, but in front.

Seen from the top. The number of joined rings increases steadily.

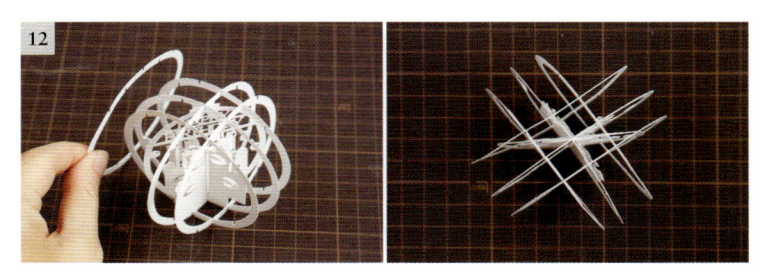

Join ring-7 parallel to ring-1, but behind it. Three rings joined vertically and horizontally in the manner of grid.

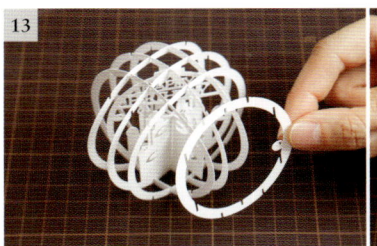

Four small rings, -8 through -11, remain. Join ring-8 parallel and in front of ring-1. Join ring-9 parallel and in front of ring-2.

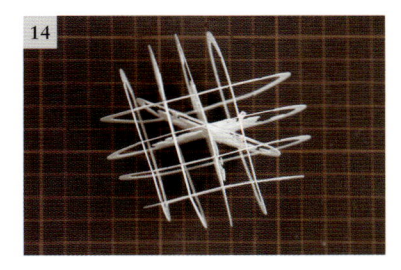

Seen from top.

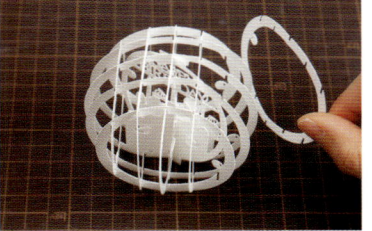

Join ring-10 parallel to ring-1, but behind. Join ring-11 parallel to ring-2, but behind. Rings-8 through -11 can be joined inverted. Position as desired.

All rings joined.

Iron on high for a few seconds to crisp up the paper.

Complete.

Join the rings crossed at center, the center motif, the outside grid (order doesn't matter). Join the outermost rings last. The outermost ring can be joined any way you want. Display the sphere facing forward or at an angle. The only thing you should pay attention to is not to invert the letters in the motifs.

Instructions: Mounting the Sphere on a Card

This section gives instructions to mount a medium-2 sphere onto a card. When the card is opened the sphere will pop up.

Prepare a medium-2 sphere and some 11.5 x 19.5 cm / 4½" x 7¾" card stock. The medium-2 sphere will fit in the card stock specified above. Choose any paper you desire, as long as the size isn't smaller than that noted above.

Fold card stock in half and make a crease using a ruler.

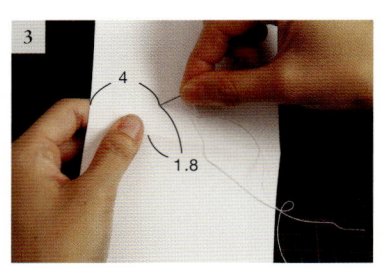

From the outside of the card, pierce a threaded needle 4 cm / 1½" in from the edge of the card and 1.8 cm / ¾" above the centerline.

Thread where the center ring and the outermost ring cross. Then, push the needle back through the initial hole.

Without cutting the thread, push the needle through 4 cm / 1½" in from the opposing edge of the card and 1.8 cm / ¾" above the centerline.

Similar to step 4, thread the needle through and then push it back. Tie off the thread.

Fold the card and make sure everything is in place.

In order to prevent the thread from loosening, secure with masking tape, etc.

Do the same for the other side of the card. Fold the card and then open to see if the sphere pops up smoothly. Secure the thread with masking tape if everything works.

Cover with decorative paper. Fold the card, then put glue on the back. Place it on the backside of the decorative paper. Leave plenty of margin around the card.

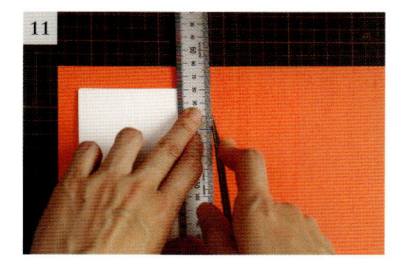

Cut the decorative paper along the folded line of the card.

Put glue on the other side of the card. Place the decorative paper on the card while aligning the folding line.

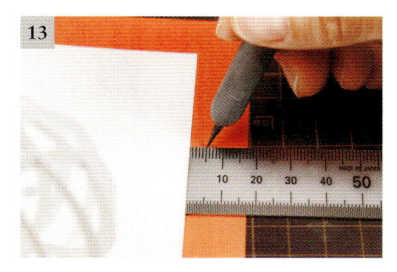

Trim around the edges of the decorative paper. Use a stylus to mark 5mm / ¼" out from the edges of the card.

Trim off using an art knife.

The decorative cover is attached. Touch up the folding line because the decorative cover doesn't extend all the way over the folding line.

Lay down some masking tape and align the card so it runs along the center. Fold the masking tape along the folding line to create a spine.

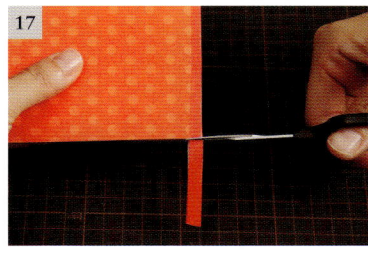

Keep the card folded. Cut off the excess tape. Then, open the card and trim.

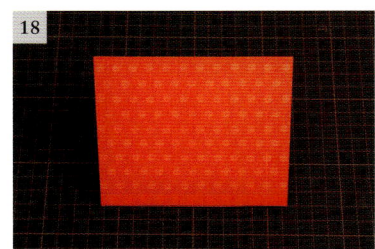
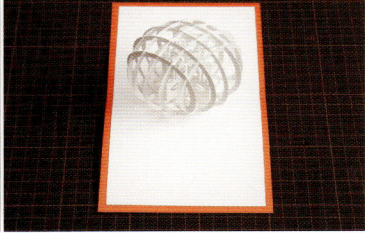

Complete. Open and close the card to make sure the sphere pops up.

Large

This section introduces the largest size sphere. The diameter of the ring is 9.8 cm / 3⅞". A large sphere is composed of twenty-two rings and, of those, four rings have motifs. The rings are joined densely together thus creating a rounder, more amusing spherical shape. One unique feature is the gate attached to the front. It is fun to look inside, as if you were opening the gate to peek in. The spherical shape is maintained, despite of large number of rings required, because of the stopper. This is a mechanism that only the large sized sphere employs.

Instructions: see p. 52

Alice's Teatime

The sphere on p. 34 has been made into a large sized sphere. Open the gate to look inside. Fun! It's like looking into a kaleidoscope.

Patterns: p. 88 ~ 93, 117 ~ 128

The rings are joined diagonally.

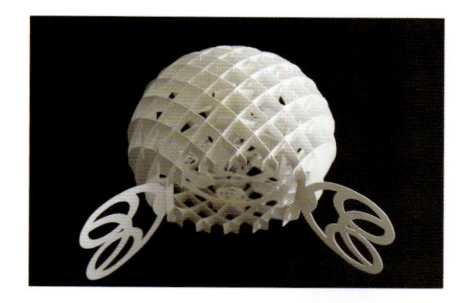

This item looks like a sphere from any angle because it has so many rings and such complexity.

Wondrously, it can still fold down flat.

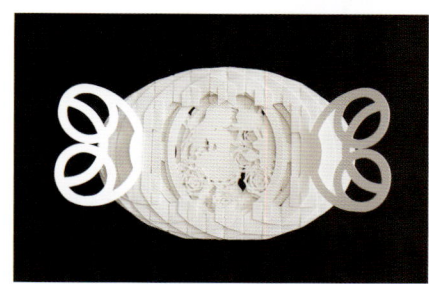

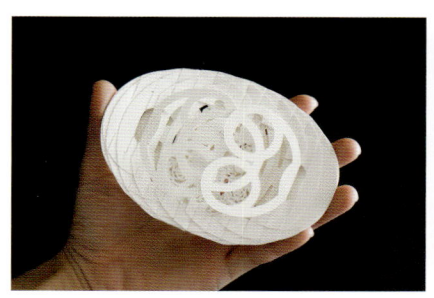  

To make the sphere shape, just push in on the sides. It will instantly become a sphere. Don't forget to open the gate!

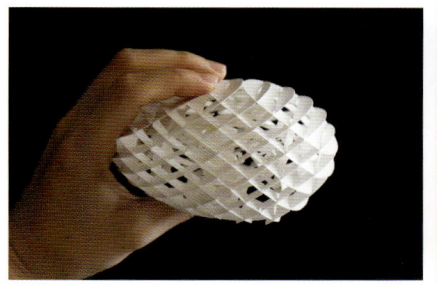 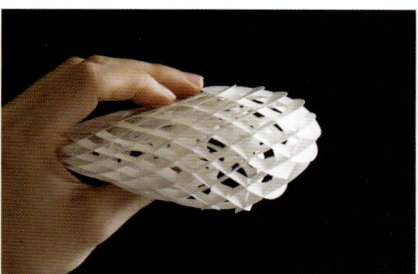 

To fold flat, close the gate and then forcefully press the top and bottom together. This will deactivate the stopper and flatten the sphere instantly.

Happy Birthday

The large size is perfect for interior decor items. The "layered cake" motifs will emerge when lit up from behind.

Patterns: p. 88 ~ 92, 94

This is a more extravagant
version of the Christmas card
on p. 25. Helps give off the
impression of a white Christmas.

Patterns: p. 88 ~ 92, 95

The number of rings is increased all at once. This makes things much more complex. First, join the rings to make a spherical shape. Then, join the rings that have the motifs. The steps for assembling are basically the same as for the other types. Begin with the center of the grid and then move in an outward direction.

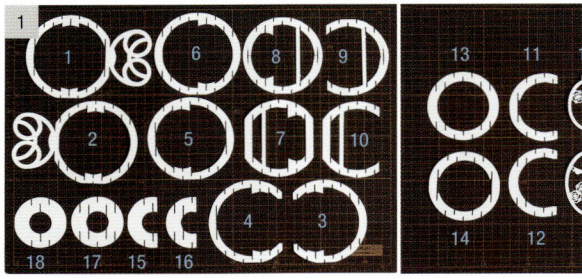

Prepare rings-1 and -2.

Requires twenty-two rings. The rings with motifs are inserted at the center of the diagonal grid made by joining nine rings, both vertically and horizontally. The gate is attached to ring-1 and ring-2, which make up the center of a grid. Rings-19 through -22 have the motifs.

Join them so that the gate faces forward.

Join ring-3, in front of ring-1, with the open part of the ring facing out.

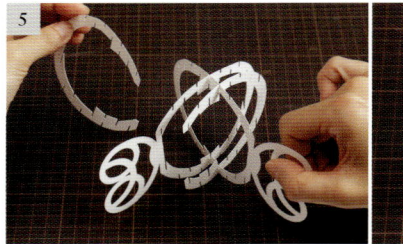
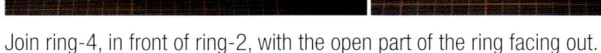

Join ring-4, in front of ring-2, with the open part of the ring facing out.

Join ring-5, behind ring-2, with the protruded notch facing down.

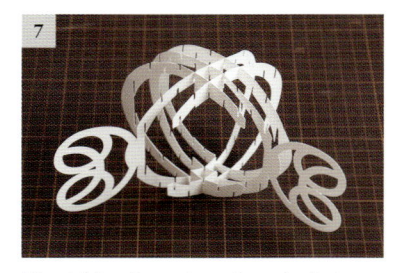
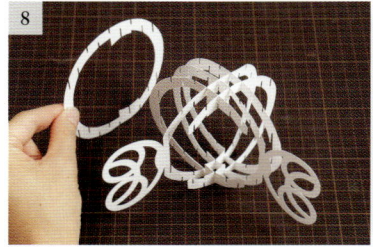

After joining these rings, the spherical shape should stabilize.

Join ring-6, behind ring-1, with the protruded notch facing down. So far three rings are joined in both diagonal directions.

 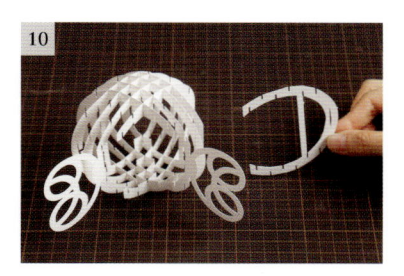

With the vertical lines facing outward, join ring-7 behind -5 and ring-8 behind -6.

Join ring-9 in front of ring-3 with the vertical line facing outward.

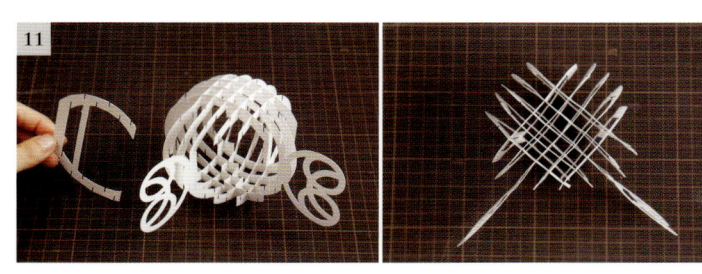 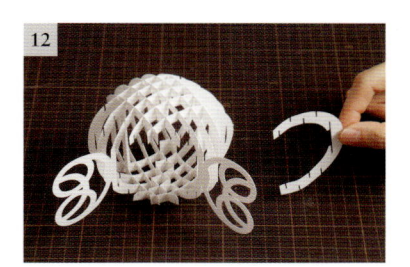

Join ring-10 in front of ring-4 with the vertical line facing outward. So far, five rings have been joined in both diagonal directions.

Similarly, with the open part of the ring facing inward, join ring-11 in front of ring-9.

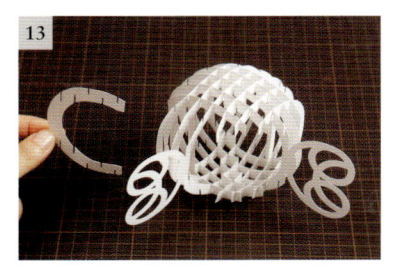 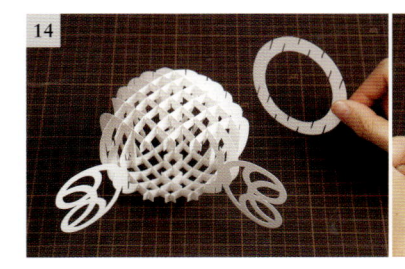

With the open part of the ring facing inward, join ring-12 in front of ring-10.

Join ring-13 behind ring-7 and join ring-14 behind ring-8.

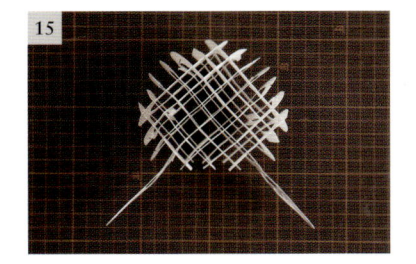 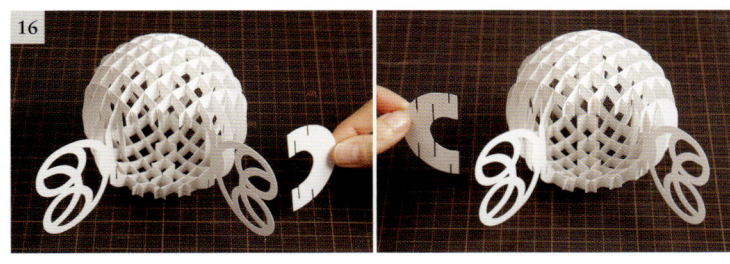

Seen from the top. Seven rings are joined in both diagonal directions.

With the open part of the rings facing inward, join -15 in front of -11 and -16 in front of -12.

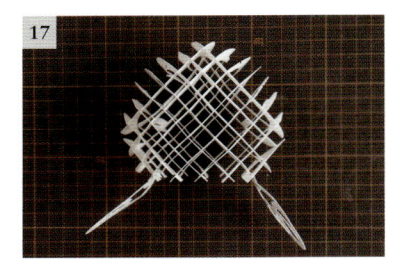

Seen from the top. The spherical shape is beginning to form.

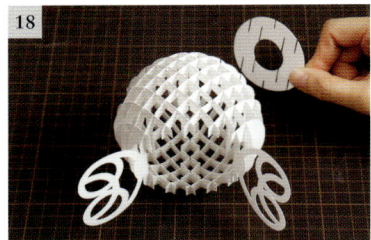
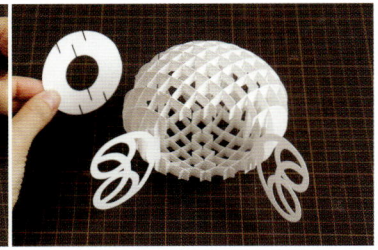

Join ring-17 behind -13 and ring-18 behind -14.

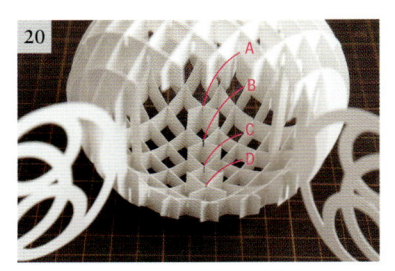

This concludes joining the rings that form a spherical shape.

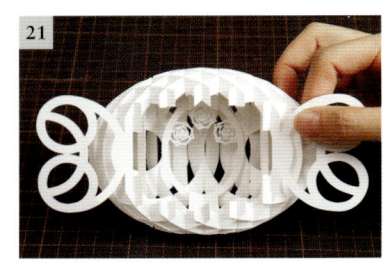

Next, insert the rings with the motifs inside the sphere. Insert each ring where the others cross. The part that is raised along the bottom center of the sphere is seen from the front. Begin at the back going from A through D.

Insert ring-19 at A. Flatten the sphere a little to make inserting the rings easier.

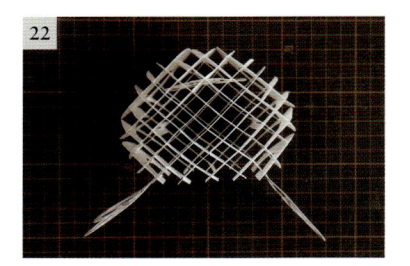

Seen from the top, one ring is inserted horizontally between the diagonals.

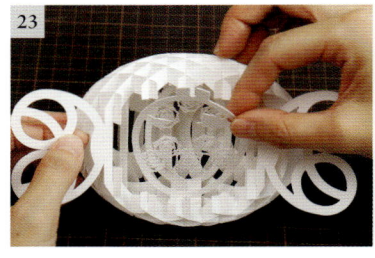

Insert ring-20 at B in a similar manner. It is easier to insert the bottom of the ring first.

Insert ring-21 at C.

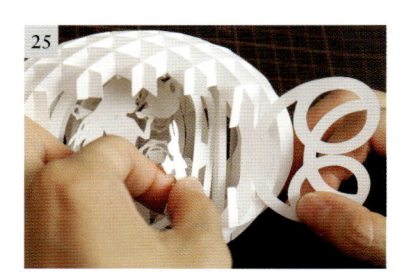

Insert one side of ring-21 between the vertical bar of rings-7 and -9 and the other side between the vertical bar of rings-8 and -10. This will create the stopper to maintain the shape of the sphere.

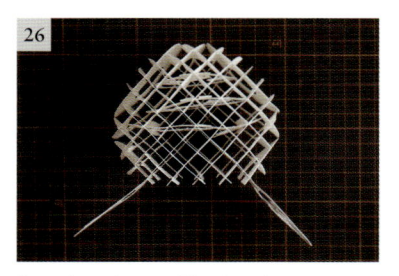

Seen from the top. The rings have the motifs lined up at equal intervals.

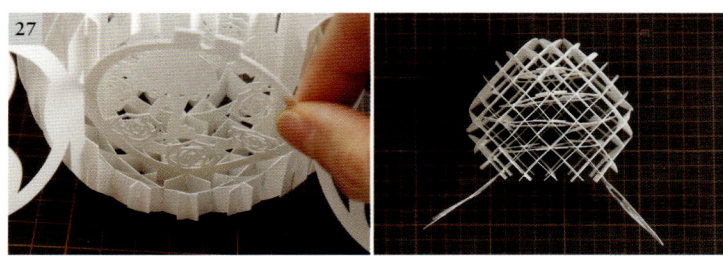

Lastly, insert ring-22 at D.

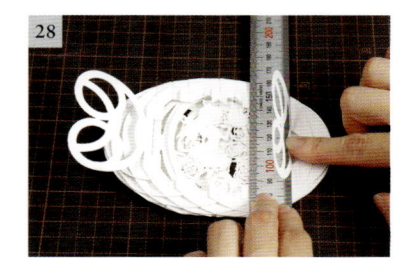

Place a ruler along the edge of the gate then fold the gate inward.

Iron on high for a few seconds to stiffen the paper.

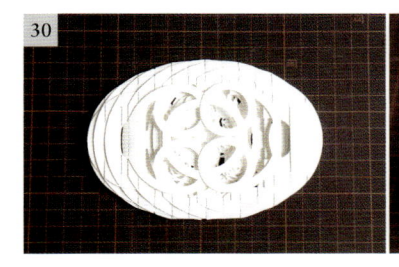

Complete.

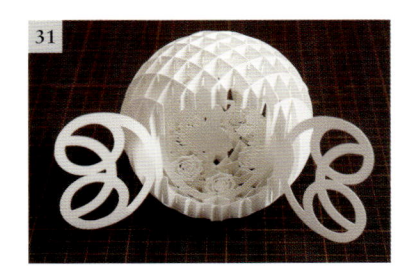

Open the gate to display.

After assembling the rings to form the spherical shape, insert the motifs. The motifs can be inverted as desired. However, many of the rings that form the sphere are not symmetrical, so make sure of the direction of each ring before joining.

An Inspiring Example

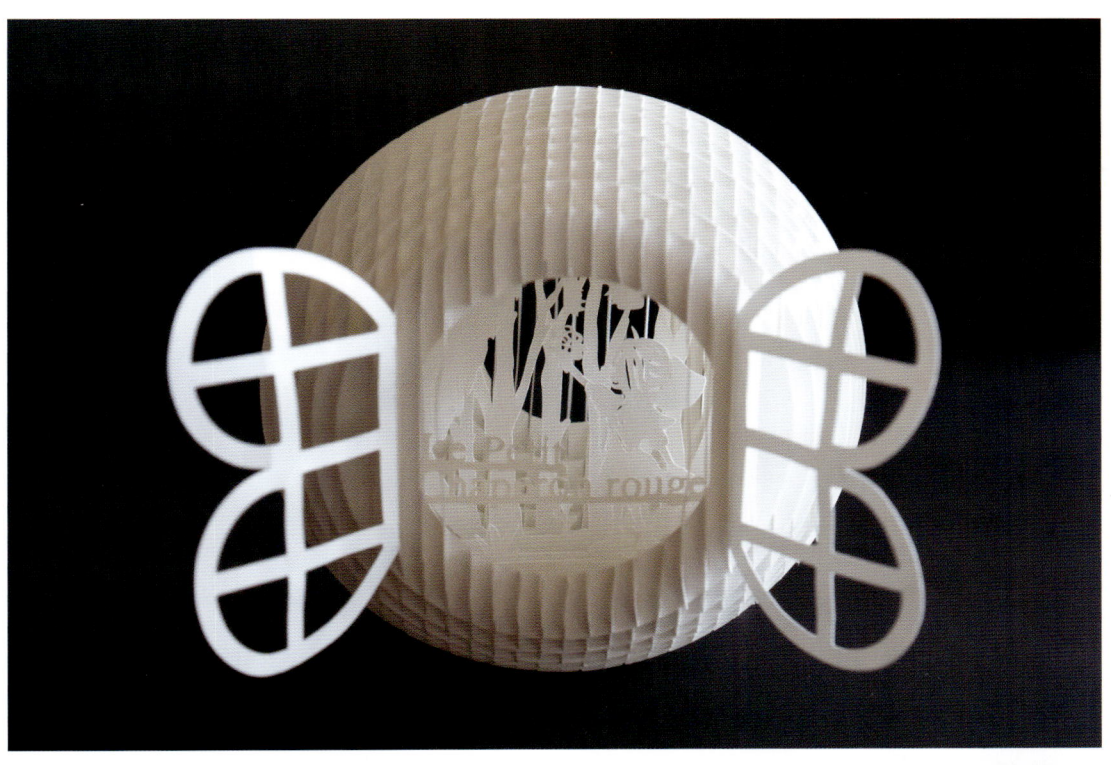

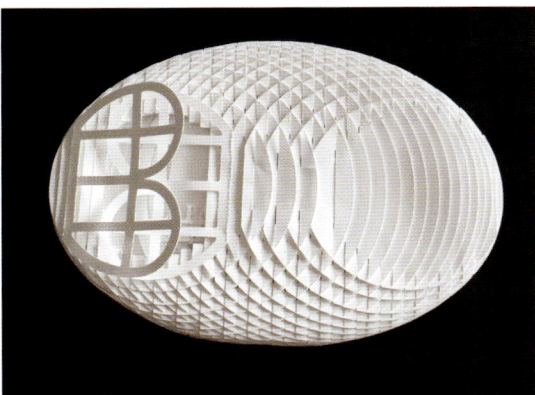
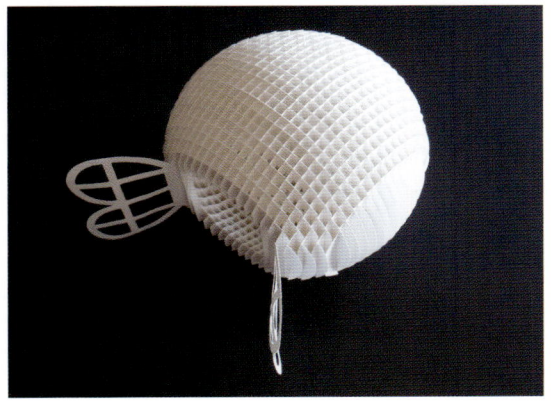

This piece is so large that it needs to be held with both hands. The rings are crossed really close together to form the wonderful sphere. I created ultra-large spheres based on this artwork.

Tools

About Tools

This section introduces tools required for making the spheres. Basically, as long as you have an art knife you can make pop-up spheres. However, there are other tools that are very convenient to have around. In addition, some tools are required when using photocopied patterns. Most tools are available at any arts and crafts store.

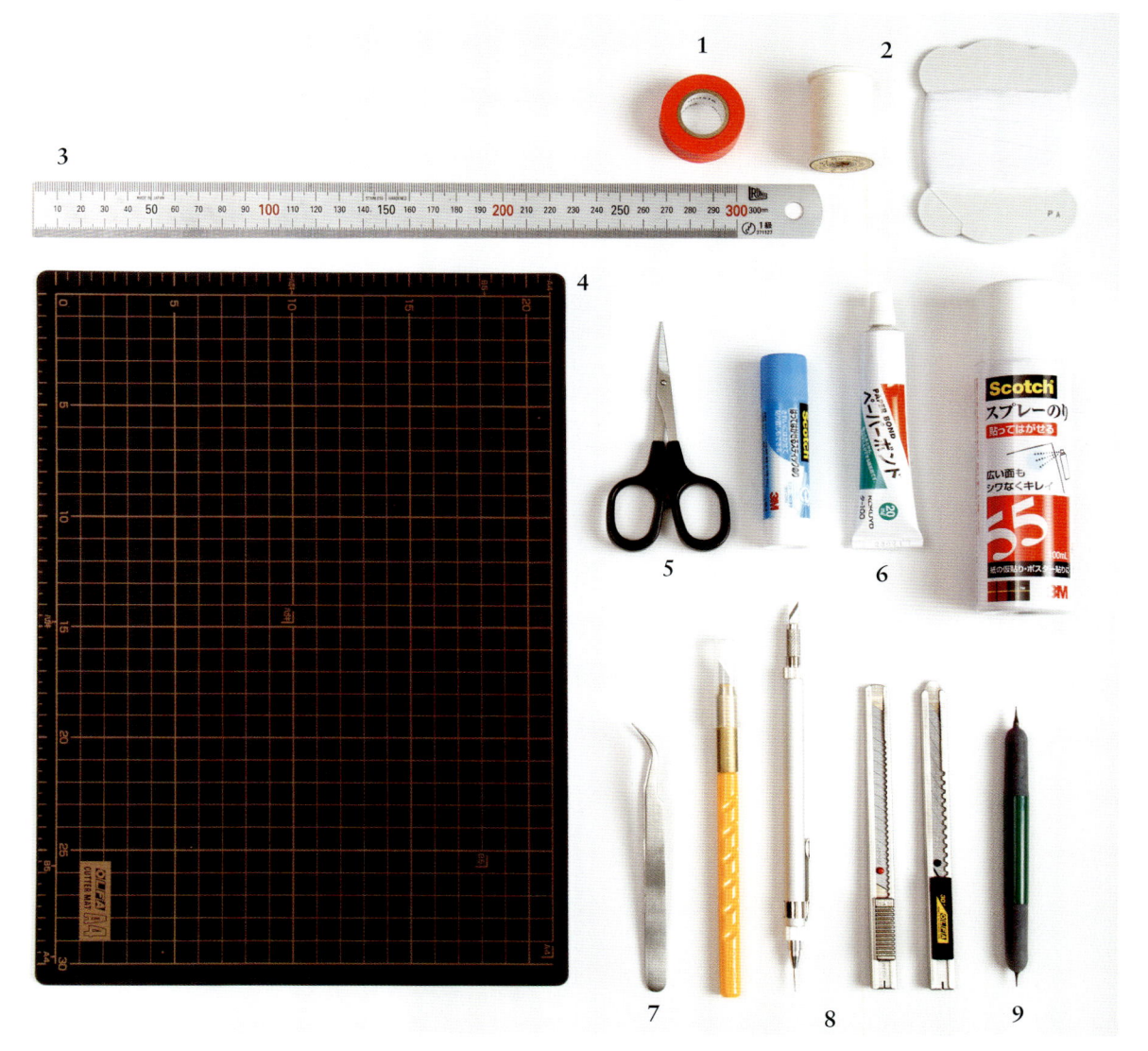

1. **Masking tape**
   To temporarily secure photocopied patterns on paper.
2. **Thread**
   Use thread to bind a sphere to a card. You'll need a sewing needle as well.
3. **Ruler**
   For cutting straight lines or creasing folded lines.
4. **Rubber mat**
   Always cut paper on a rubber mat. This will prevent scratches and knife blades will last a lot longer.
5. **Scissors**
   For convenience, use regular scissors along with sharp pointed scissors for cutting out more detailed sections.
6. **Glue**
   To temporarily secure photocopied patterns on paper. Use a removable type of glue. You can choose among a stick, the spray type or a tube.
7. **Tweezers**
   For intricate work. Use tweezers to remove cut-out rings.
8. **Art knife**
   It is preferable to use an art knife but regular box cutters will work too. Some art knives have a sharp, pointy, blade. The art knife second from left (photo above) has a blade on one end and a needle on the other.
9. **Stylus**
   For piercing holes.

Paper

About Paper

210 gsm paper is suitable for making the spheres. The thickness of paper increases as the gsm increases. The thicker the paper, the harder it is to cut. So, as a rule of thumb, 210 gsm is the thickest paper you should use. In order to enjoy your spheres from various angles, be sure to use paper where the back side and front side are not obviously different. I recommend Kent paper. Try out different types of paper and find the one that you prefer.

1. High-quality paper, 210 gsm
2. Drawing paper, 186 gsm
3. Kent paper, 210 gsm
4. Copier paper, 100 gsm
5. A sheet of drawing paper from a drawing paper pad, 128 gsm

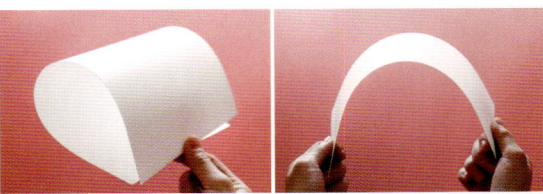

Choose paper that is similar in weight to those listed above. Be careful when handling creased and folded sheets of drawing paper as the creased/folded areas are weaker than normal.

Instructions:

Cutting Rings

Use the patterns provided from p. 97 onward. Directly cut out the patterns and construct each sphere. As for the patterns provided from p. 66 ~ 95, make photocopies of them and paste them on a sheet of your chosen paper to make "Spheres." This section presents tricks for cutting the patterns out and methods for using the patterns after photocopying them. The instructions primarily make use of an art knife. However, regular scissors can be used to cut anything outside of the rings. An art knife is definitely recommended for cutting out anything intricate.

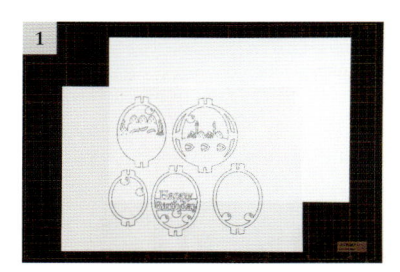

Prepare card stock and photocopies of the patterns. The card stock should be larger than the paper that contains the photocopied patterns.

Put some removable glue on the back side of the photocopied patterns. Do not add too much glue as this is only to prevent the paper from becoming misaligned. If you use stick glue, do not apply over the entire surface. Instead, just apply it to the corners.

Paste the photocopied patterns on the card stock. Neatly paste and try not to create any wrinkles.

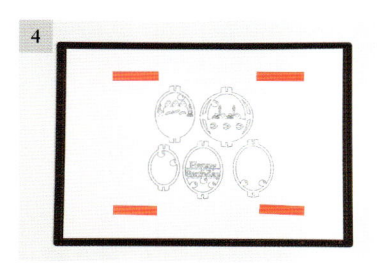

Secure all four corners with masking tape.

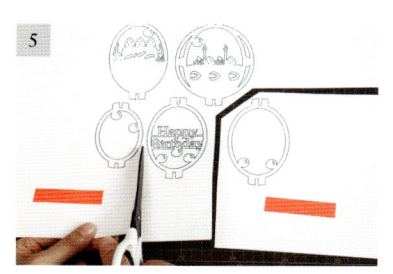

Separate each ring from the others by cutting. This will make cutting out each individual ring shape easier because the paper often needs to be moved in a circular motion to cut the angles.

Begin cutting inside the ring. Insert the blade of an art knife into a corner and then start cutting. Hold the paper down, but do not place your hand near where you will be cutting with the art knife.

Move the blade cautiously as you turn the paper in easy to cut angles. Some pressure must be applied to the blade because the card stock is a bit thick. However, applying excess pressure makes cutting difficult.

Make sure you finish cutting where you began, right in one of the corners.

Use tweezers to remove the small, cut out, piece of paper.

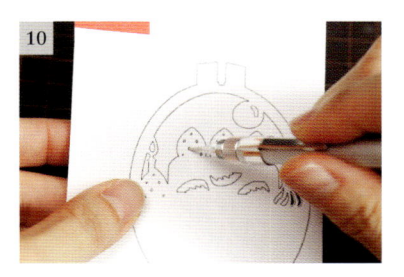

For very detailed parts, such as strawberry seeds, just pierce holes using a needle or stylus. A tack would also work.

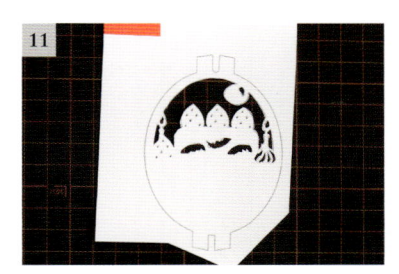

The inside is cut out.

Next, cut along the circumference of the ring. Insert the blade and create sharp corners.

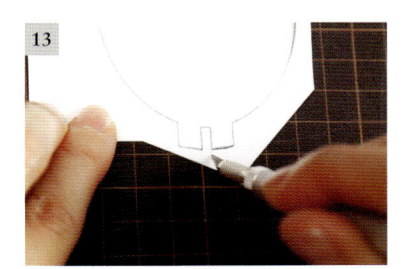

Cut off excess paper as desired.

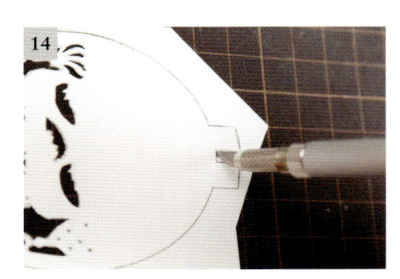

To cut neat corners remove the blade and rotate the paper then insert the blade again and cut the neighboring line.

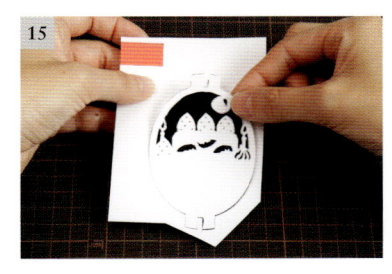

Once all of the lines are cut, push the ring forward to remove.

Adjust crooked lines using scissors or an art knife.

Carefully peel off the photocopied pattern that was glued on the card stock.

If some of the glue remains, use a little masking tape or some rubber that is exclusively for removing glue. Cut out the remaining patterns.

Patterns

On the following pages are patterns for all spheres presented in this book. As instructed on p. 60, make photocopies of these patterns and paste them on card stock to make your spheres. Instead of using photocopies of the patterns, you could also trace the pattern onto card stock to transfer it. However, make sure to keep your tracing lines as light as possible so they aren't distracting.

Patterns for a select six spheres can be found beginning on p. 97. These patterns, printed on card stock, are ready to be cut directly out of the page and used as is. Many of the spheres don't have a specific front and back, but the side of the pattern that has the printing on it should face the back. That is, the patterns are printed as inverted images. So, when you are constructing your spheres make sure the white side is facing you.

As a reminder, the instructions can be found on p. 18 for small, p. 28 for medium-1, p. 42 for medium-2, and p. 52 for large.

These are the rings used for small sized spheres. Except for the two rings at the center, all small sized cards use these five rings.
See p. 18 for instructions.

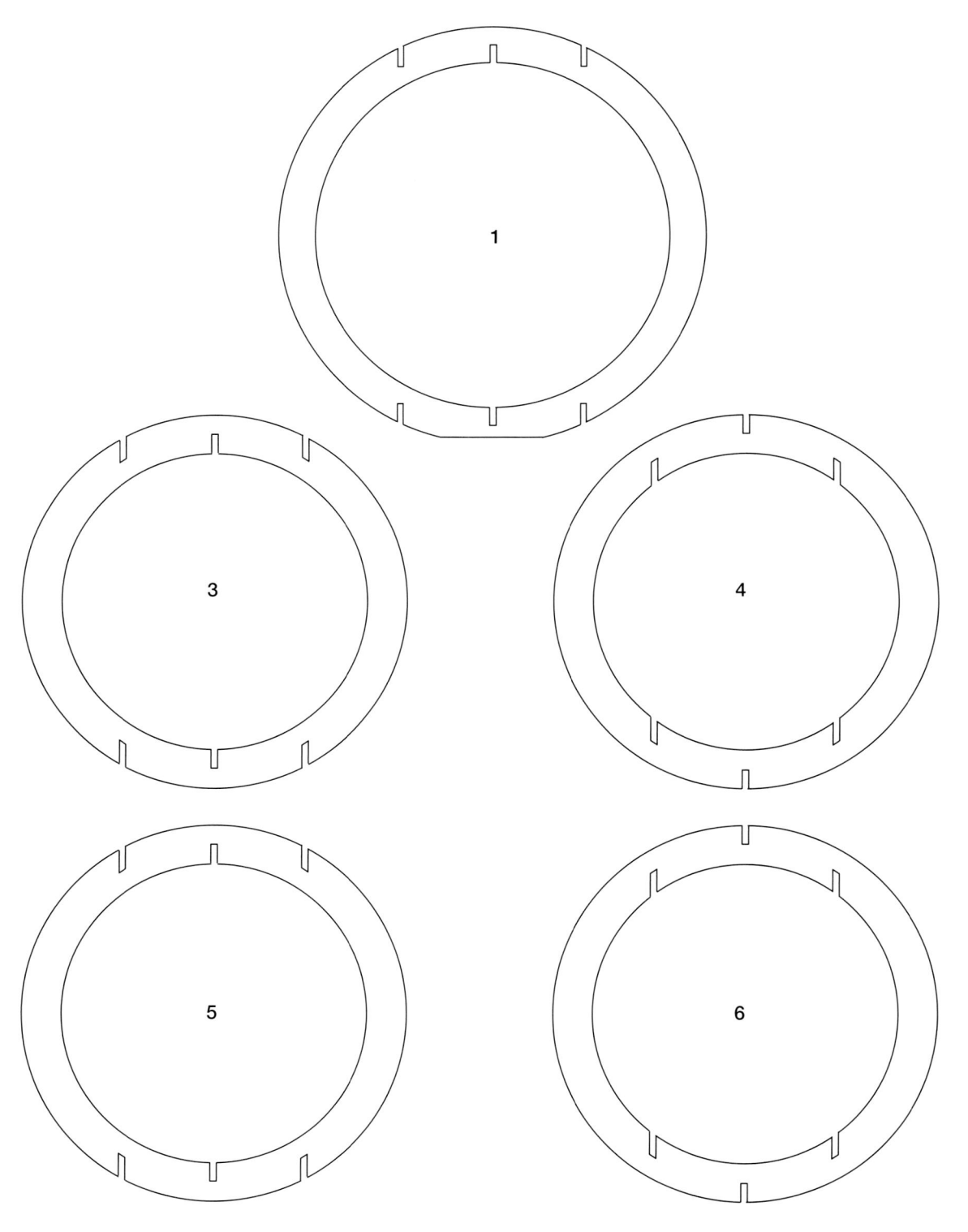

These are the motifs at the center of the small cards (ring-2 in the instructions).
See p. 18 for instructions.

These are the motifs at the center of the small cards (ring-2 in the instructions).
See p. 18 for instructions.

These are the motifs at the center of the small cards (ring-2 in the instructions).
See p. 18 for instructions.

Cherry Blossom

Rose

Three Stars

Snowflake

Christmas Tree

These are the motifs at the center of the small cards (ring-2 in the instructions).
See p. 18 for instructions.

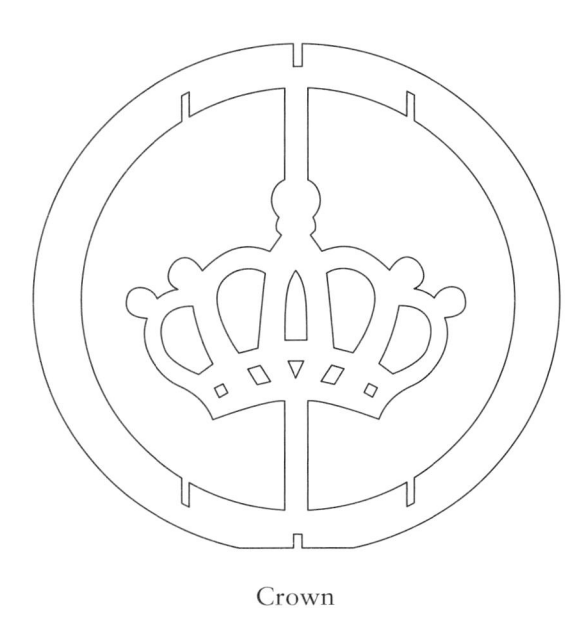

Crown

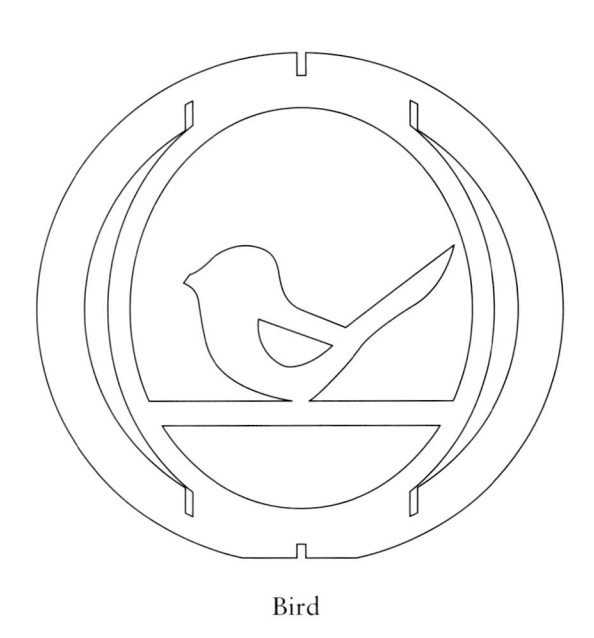

Bird

Four-leaf Clover

Hearts

These are the same rings as for medium-1. All of the rings required, except -3, -8, and -9 (which make the motif at the center), are common use with medium-1. Use the six rings on p. 71 and 72. See p. 28 for instructions.

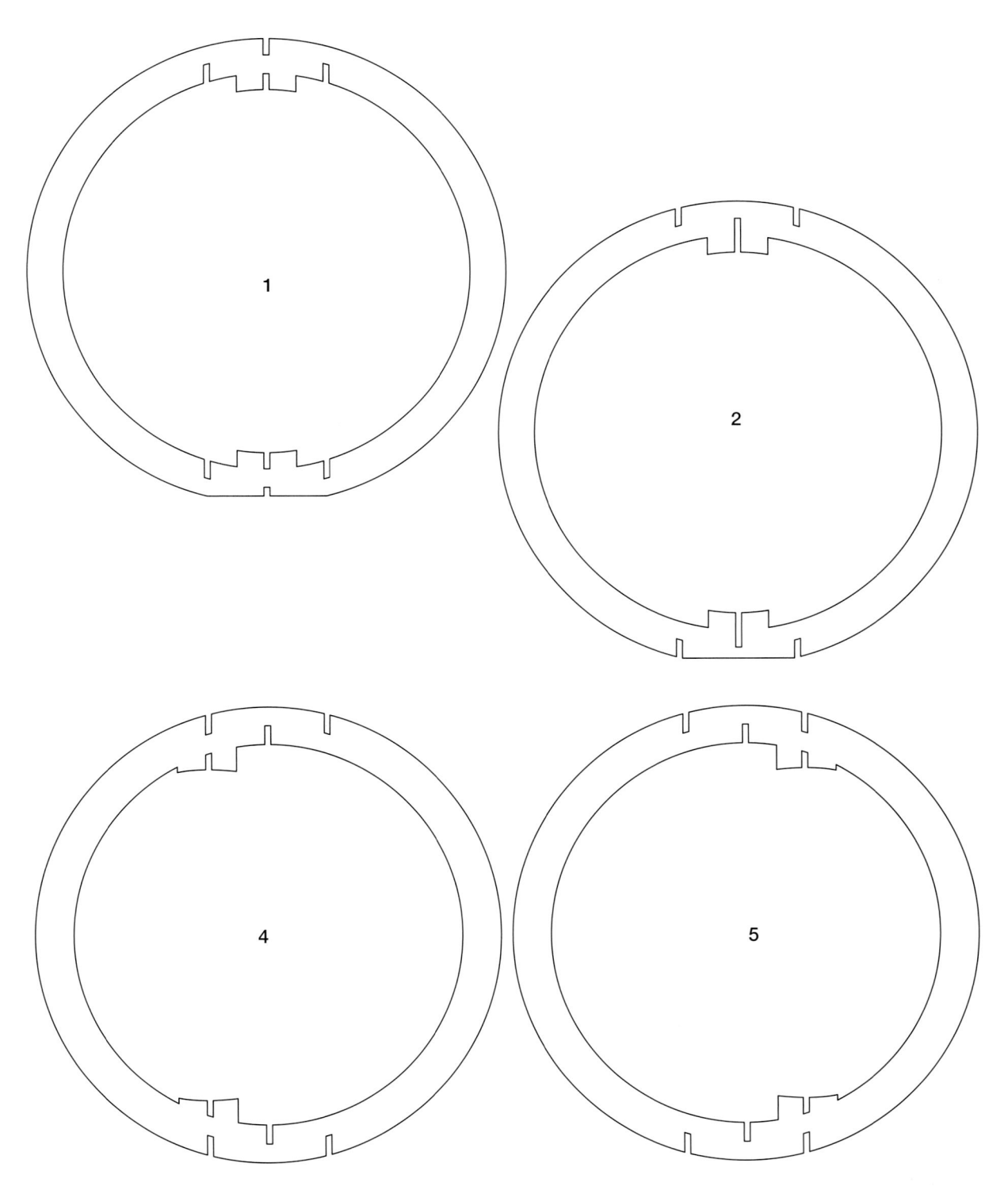

These are the same rings as for medium-1. The top two rings are the common rings. Use them with the rings found on p. 71. The bottom three rings are the motif for the Happy Birthday Card. They will be inserted at center.

See p. 28 for instructions.

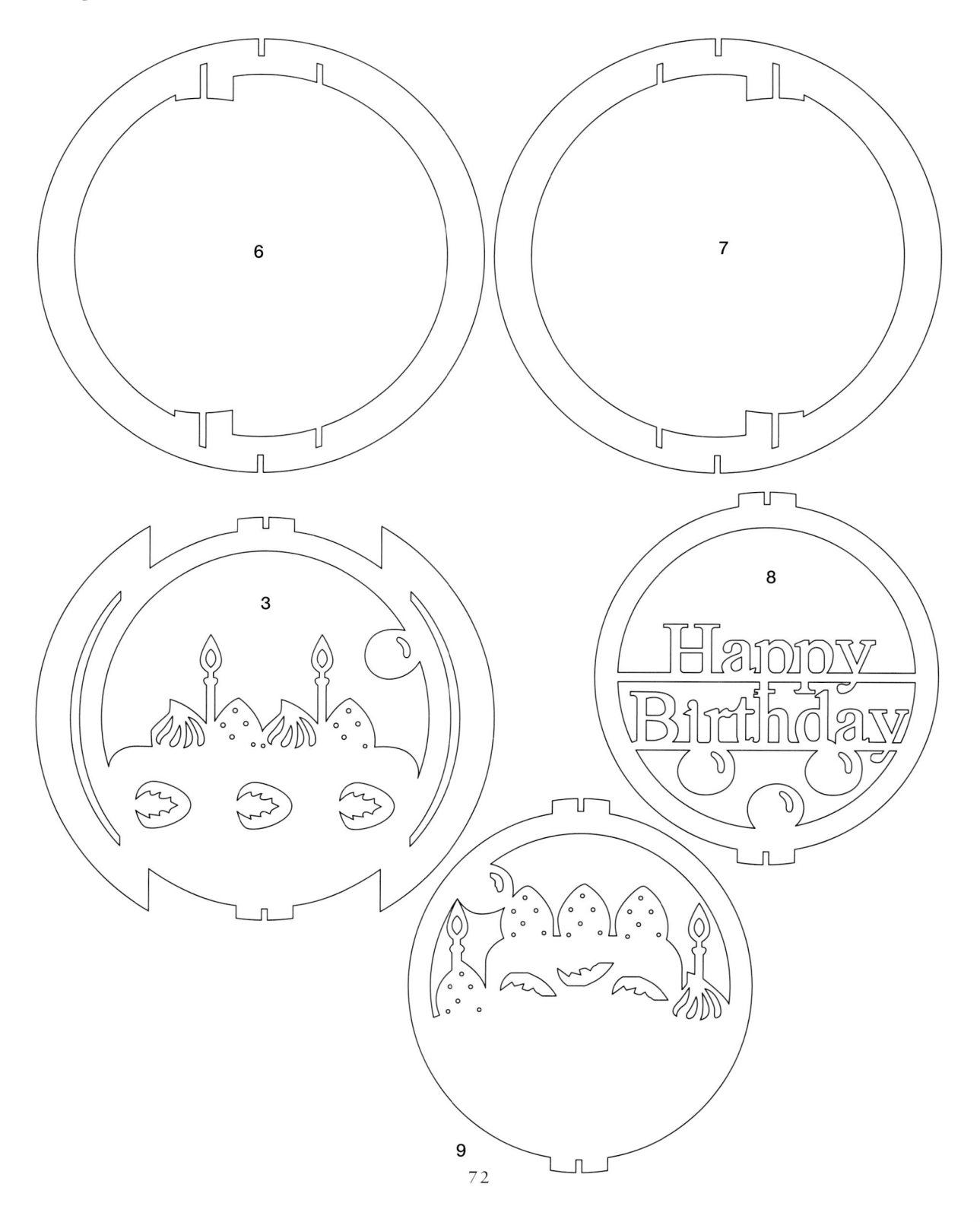

These are the motif rings for the medium-1 sized card — Present.
See p. 28 for instructions.

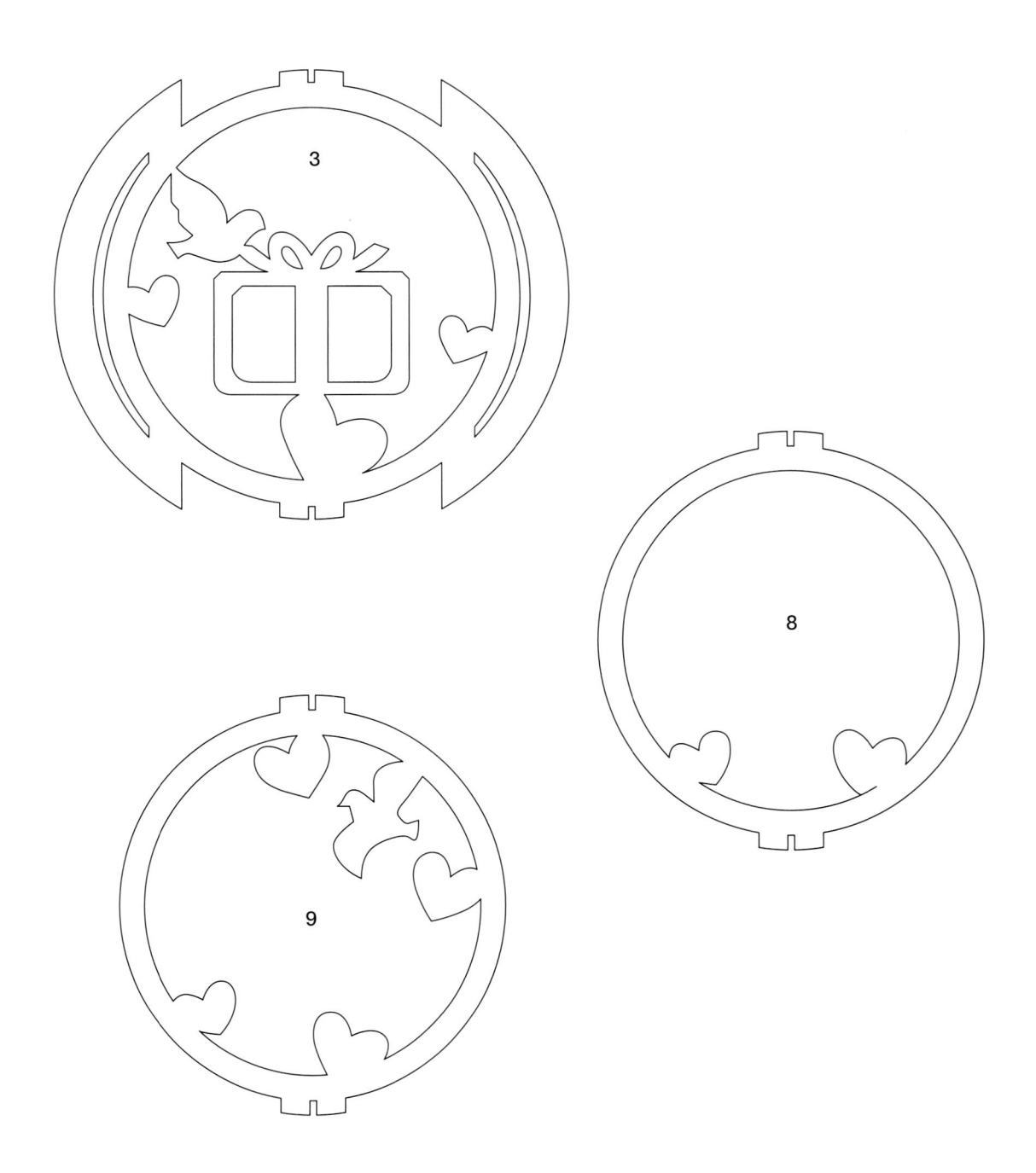

These are the motif rings for the medium-1 sized card — Halloween.
See p. 28 for assembling instructions.

These are the motif rings for the medium-1 sized card — Merry Christmas.
See p. 28 for instructions.

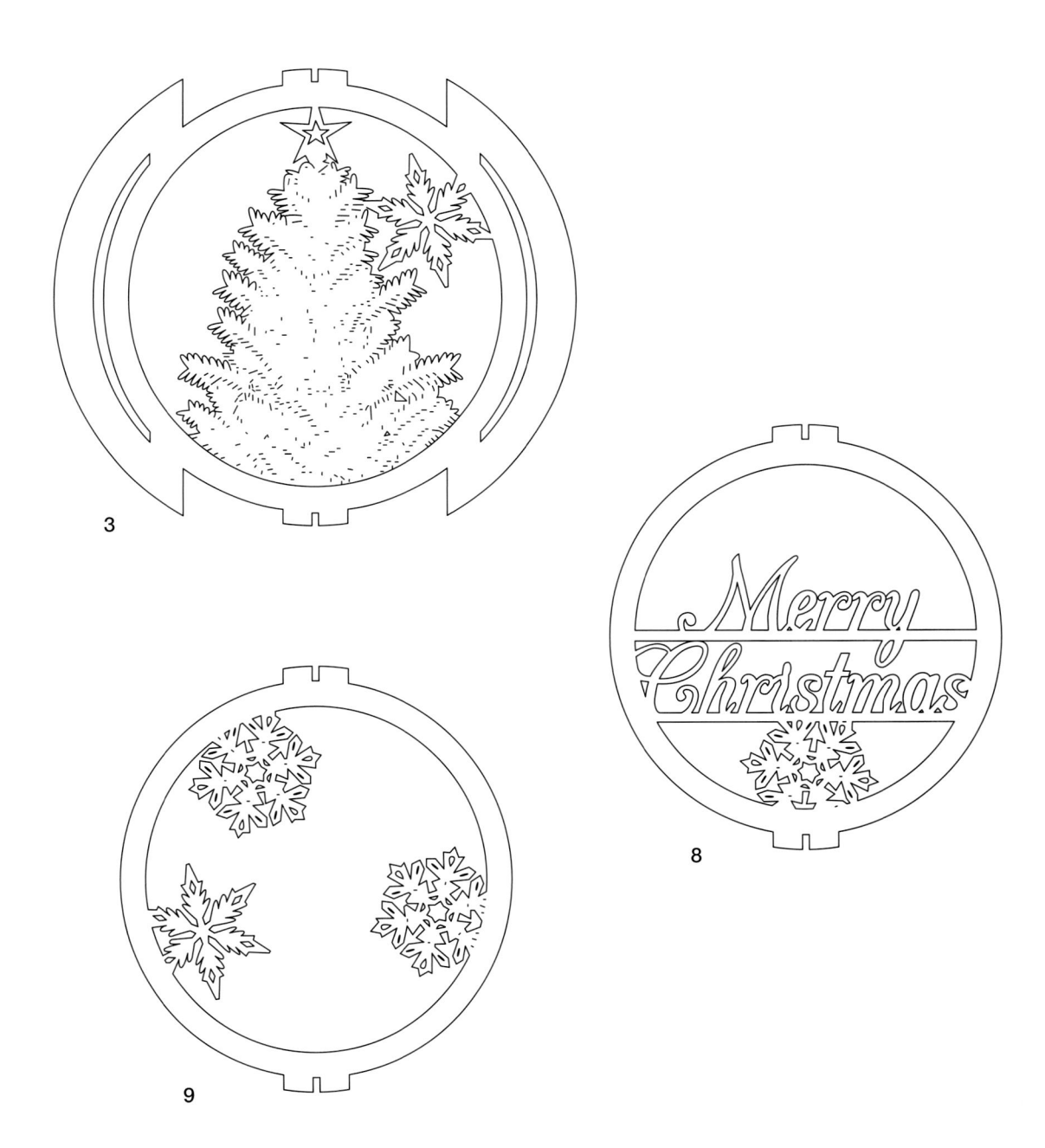

These are the motif rings for the medium-1 sized card — Lily of the Valley and Fairy.
See p. 28 for instructions.

3

8

9

These are the rings used for medium-2. They are the rings that are joined next to the motif. The motif rings won't be inserted between these four rings. These four rings are used in all medium-2 sized cards, so be sure to cut out all four.
See p. 42 for instructions.

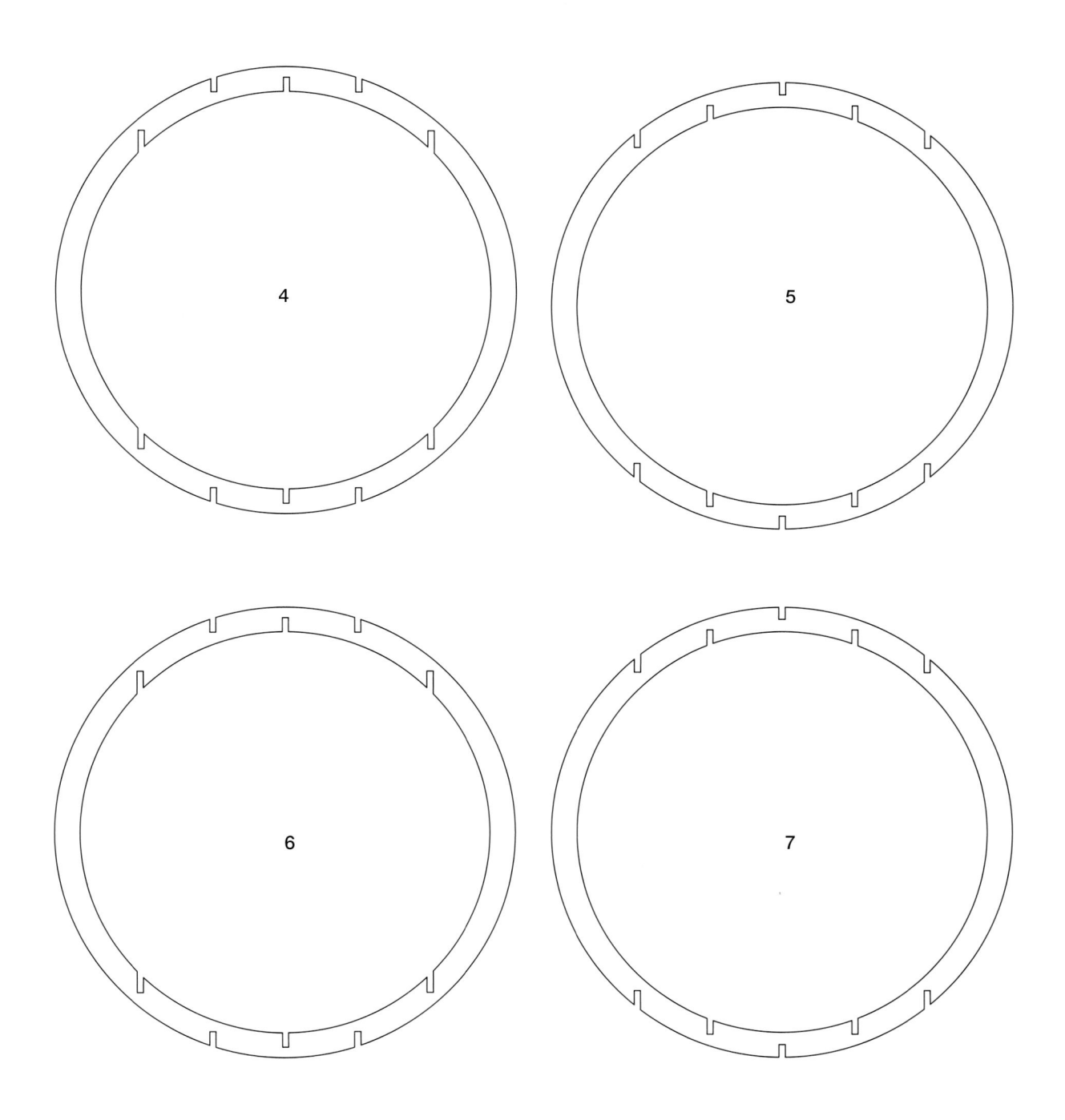

These are the seven rings that have the medium-2 sized card motif — Wedding.
See p. 42 for instructions.

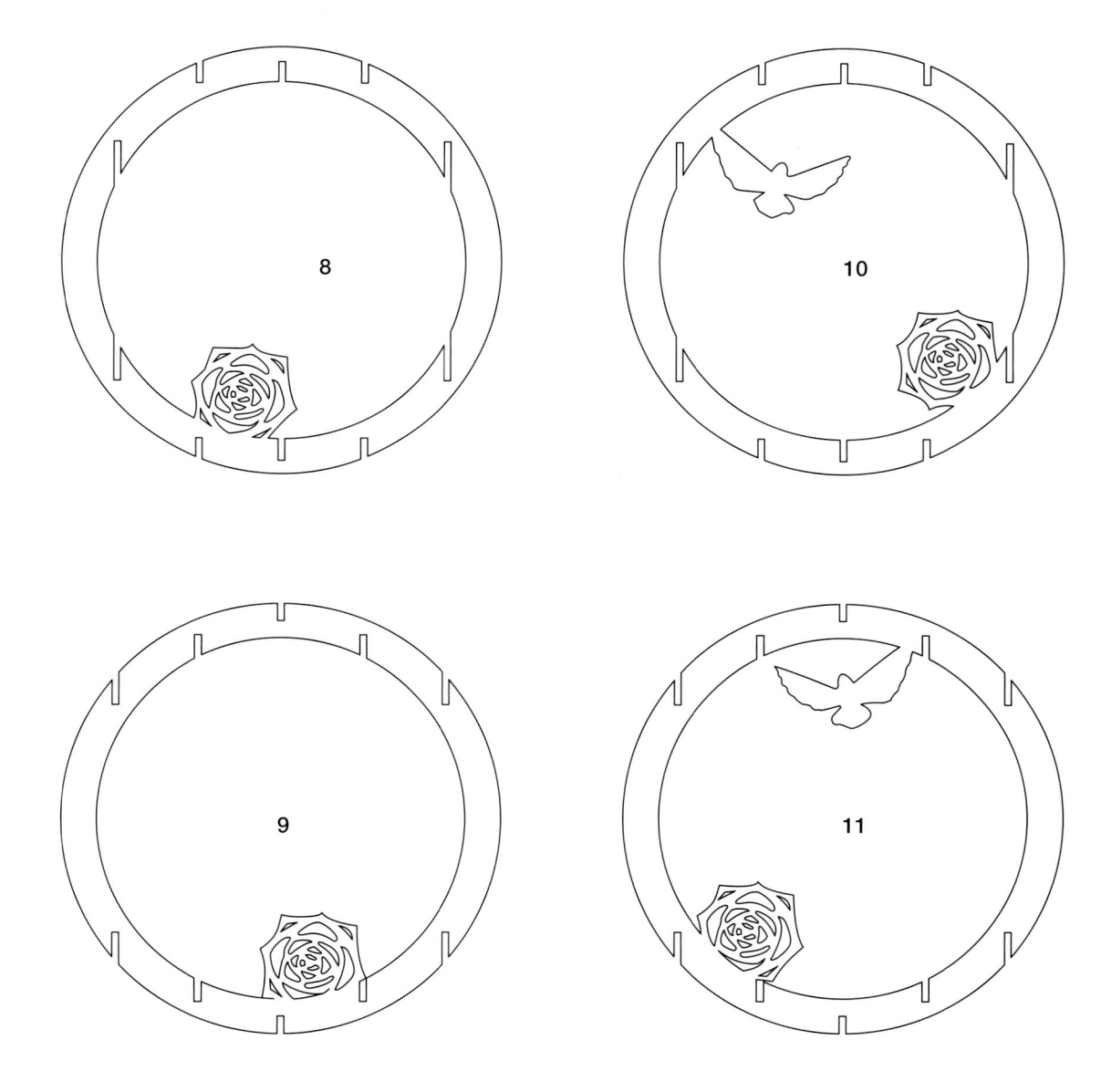

Patterns for medium-2: Five rings have motifs and two do not.
See p. 42 for instructions.

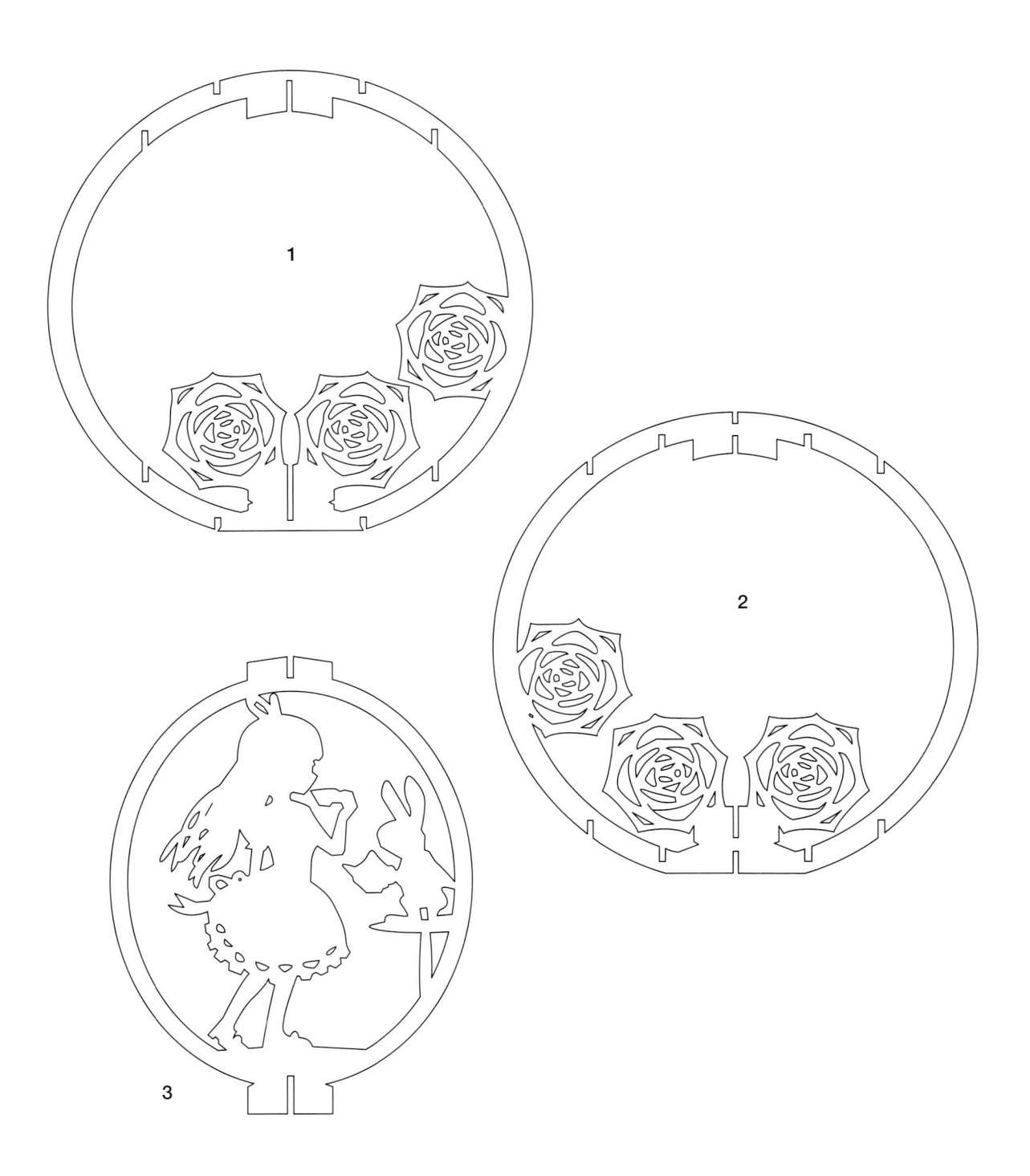

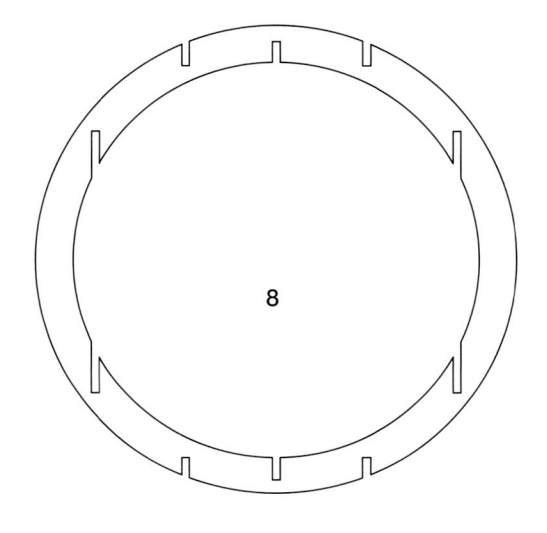

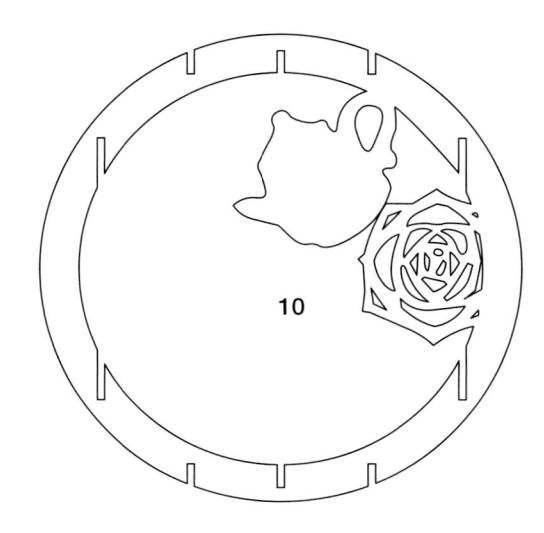

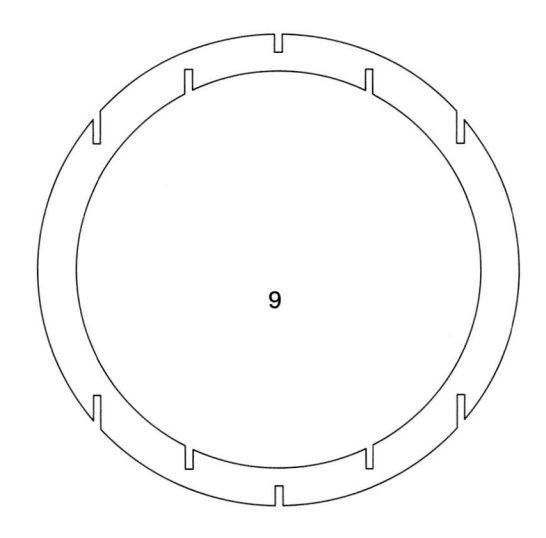

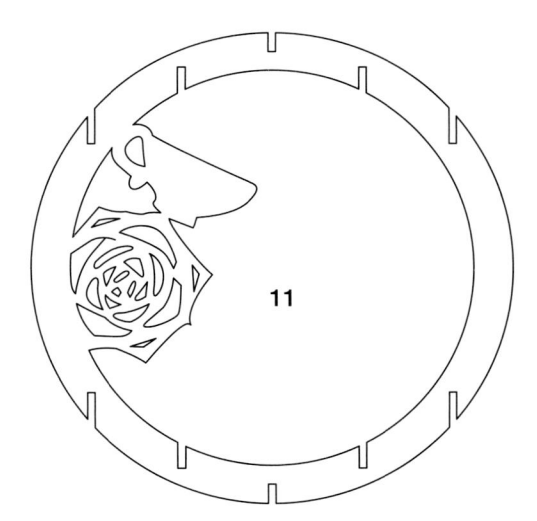

Patterns for medium-2: Five rings have motifs and two do not.
See p. 42 for instructions.

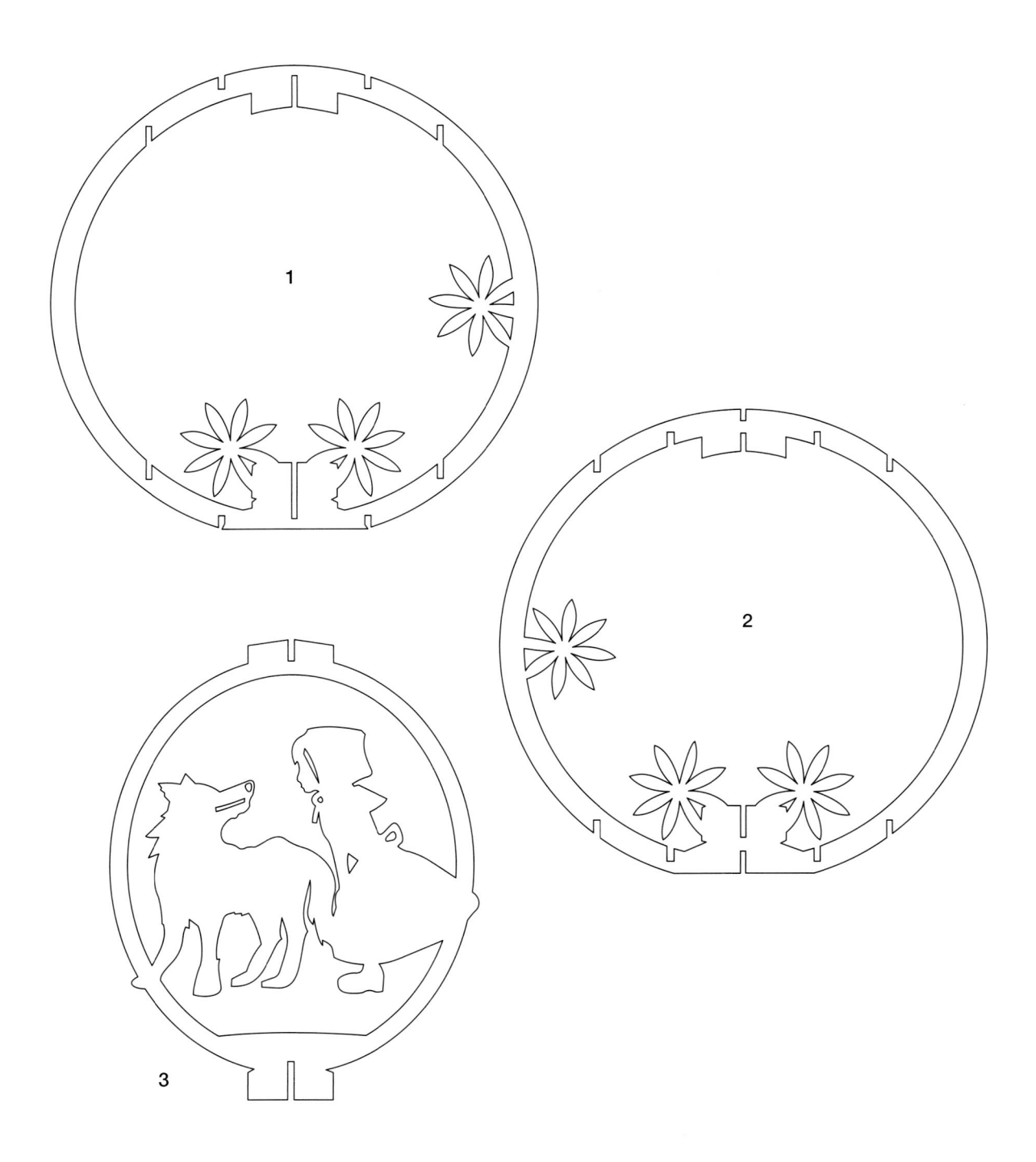

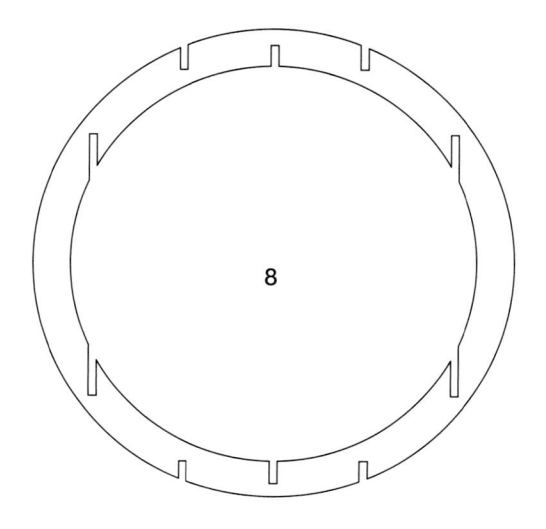

8

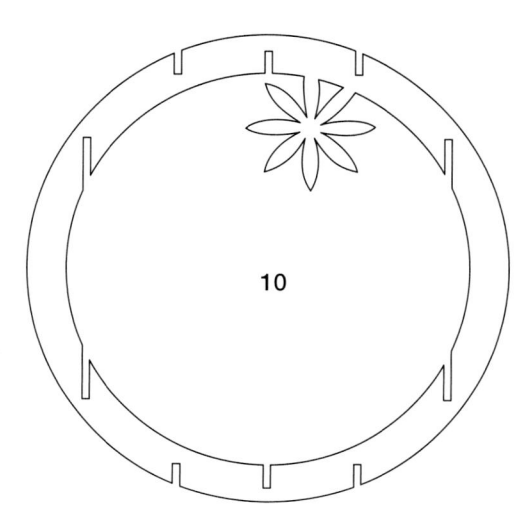

10

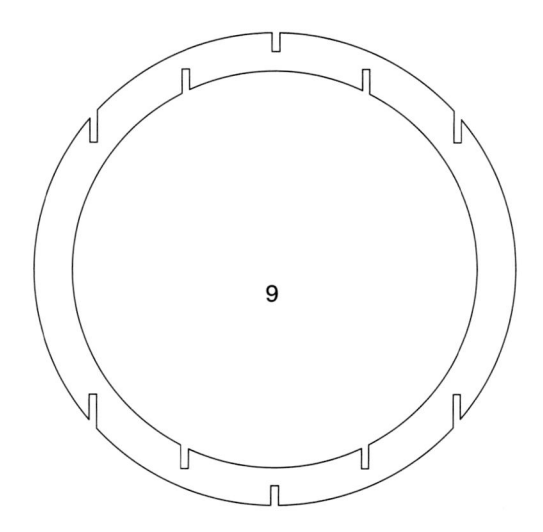

9

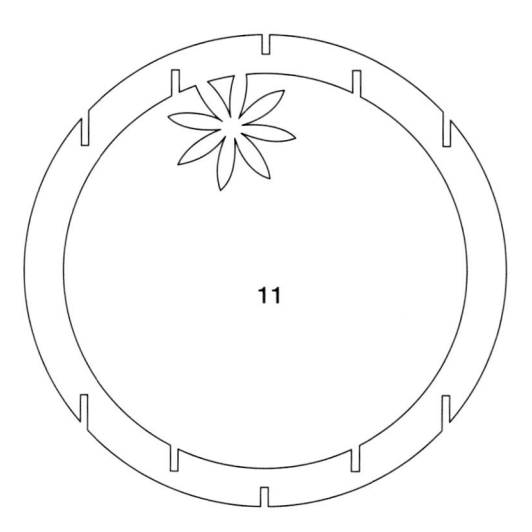

11

Patterns for medium-2: Five rings have motifs and two do not.
See p. 42 for instructions.

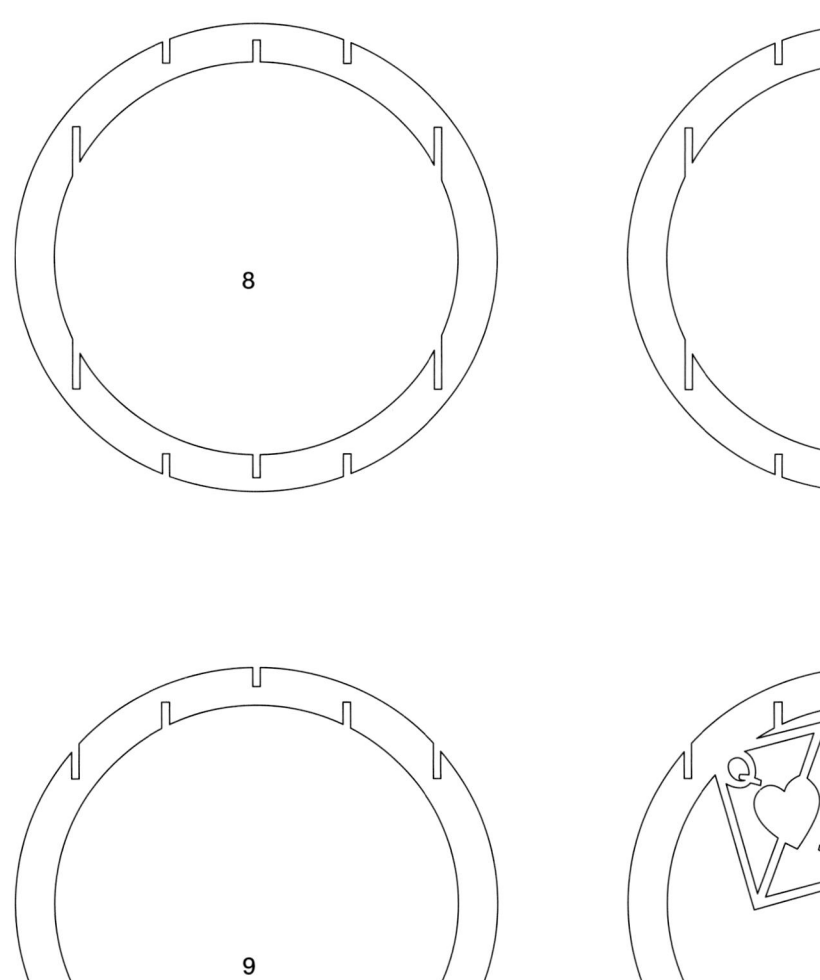

8

10

9

11

Patterns for medium-2: Seven rings have motifs.
See p. 42 for instructions.

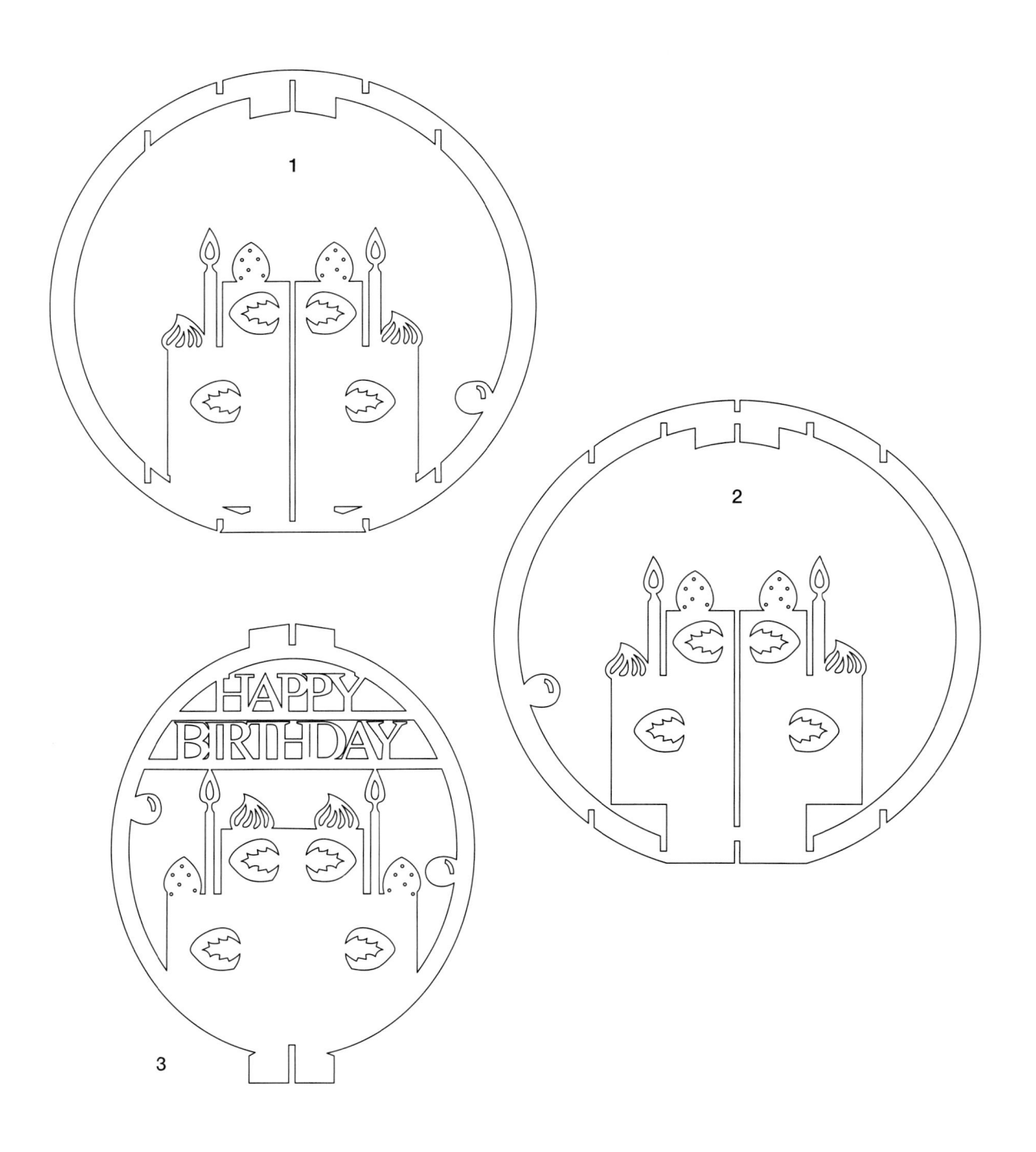

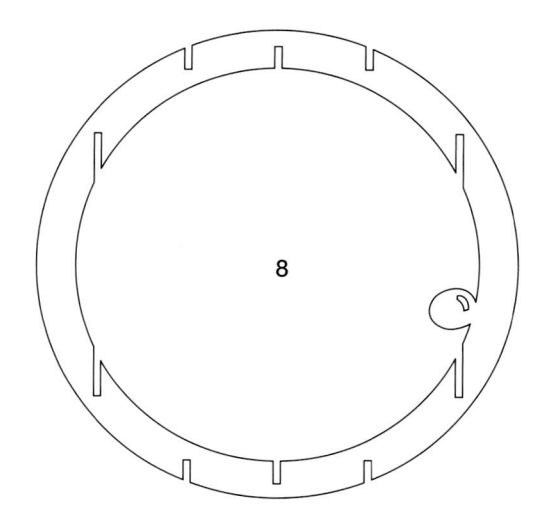

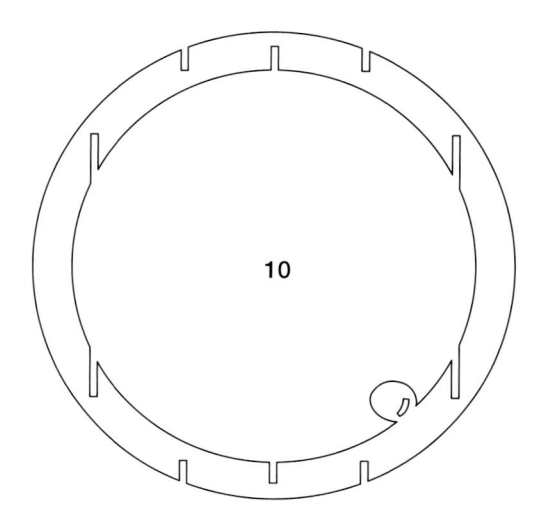

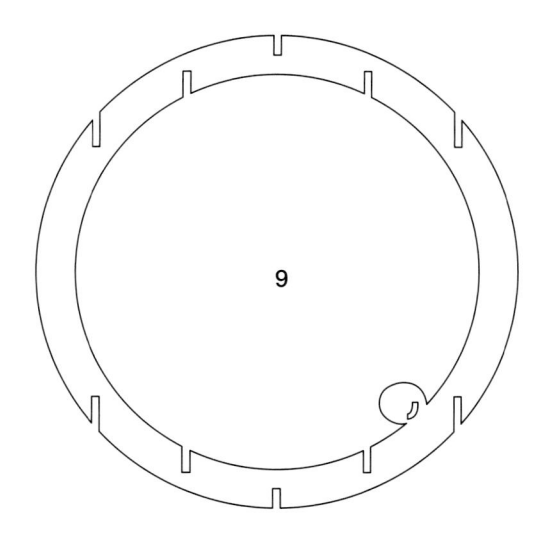

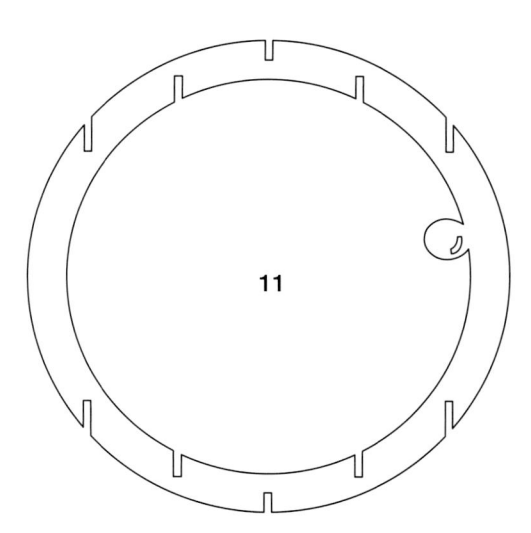

These are the rings for large sized spheres. Aside from the four rings for the center motif, the rest of the rings are common. Use the rings presented on p. 88 ~ 92.
See p. 52 for instructions.

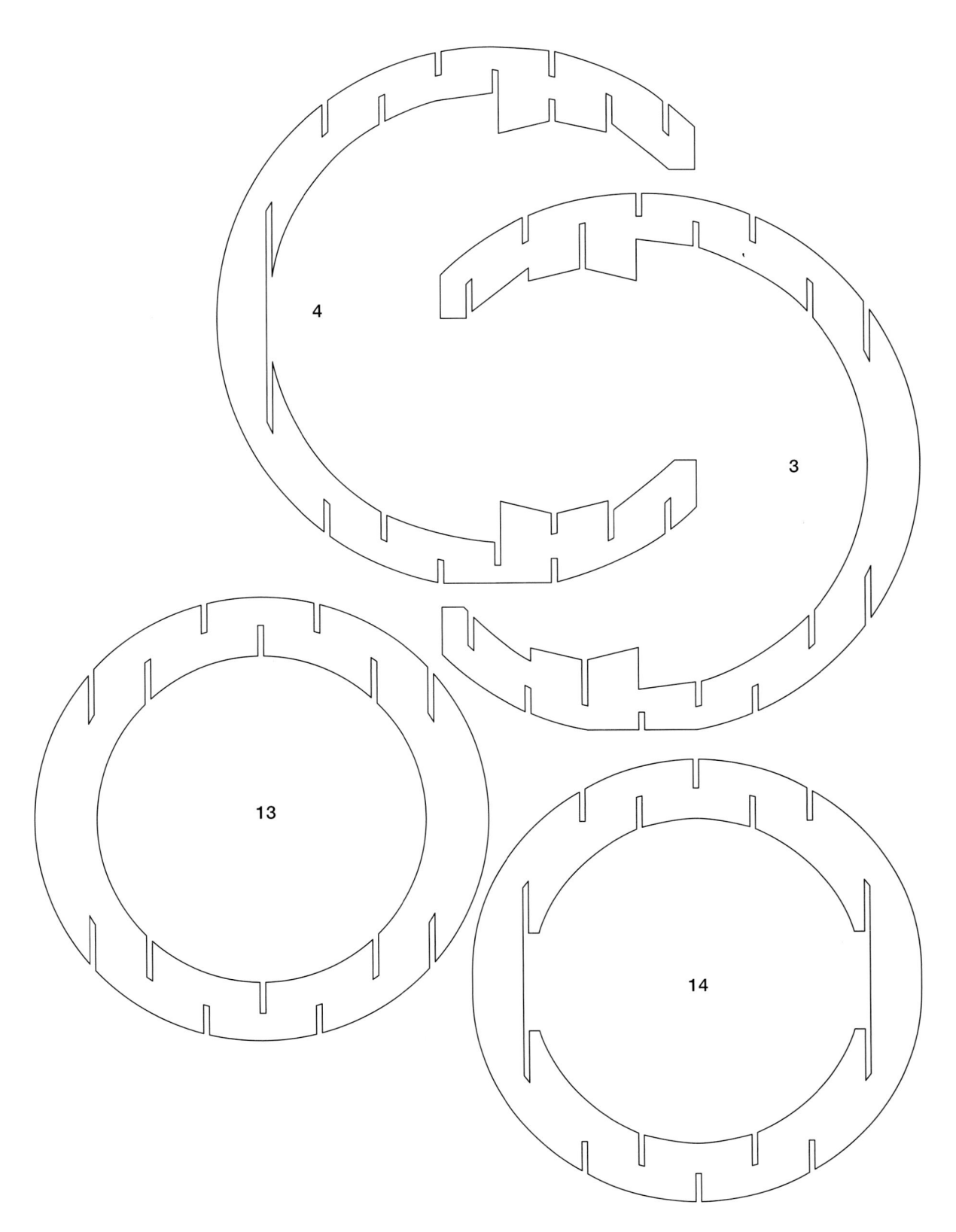

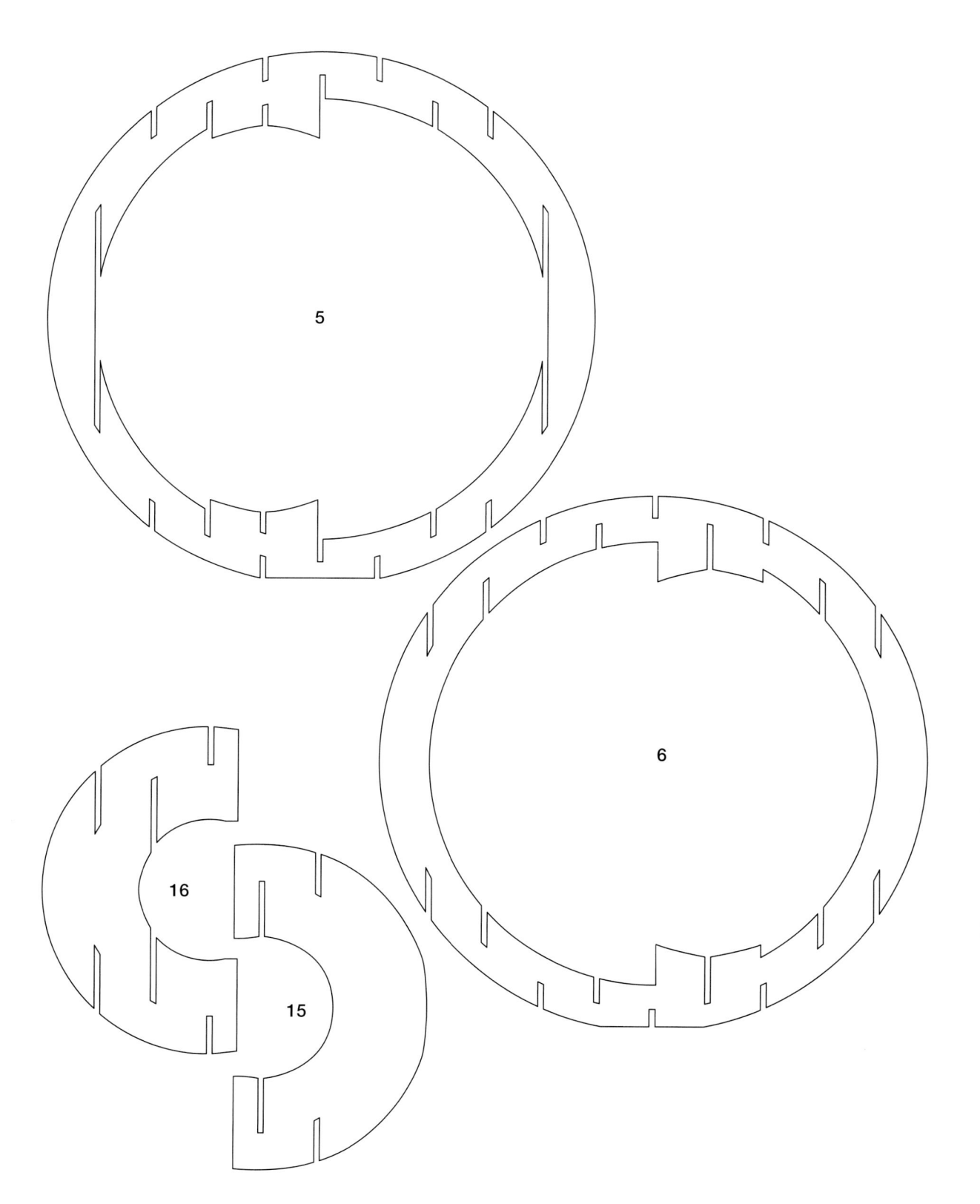

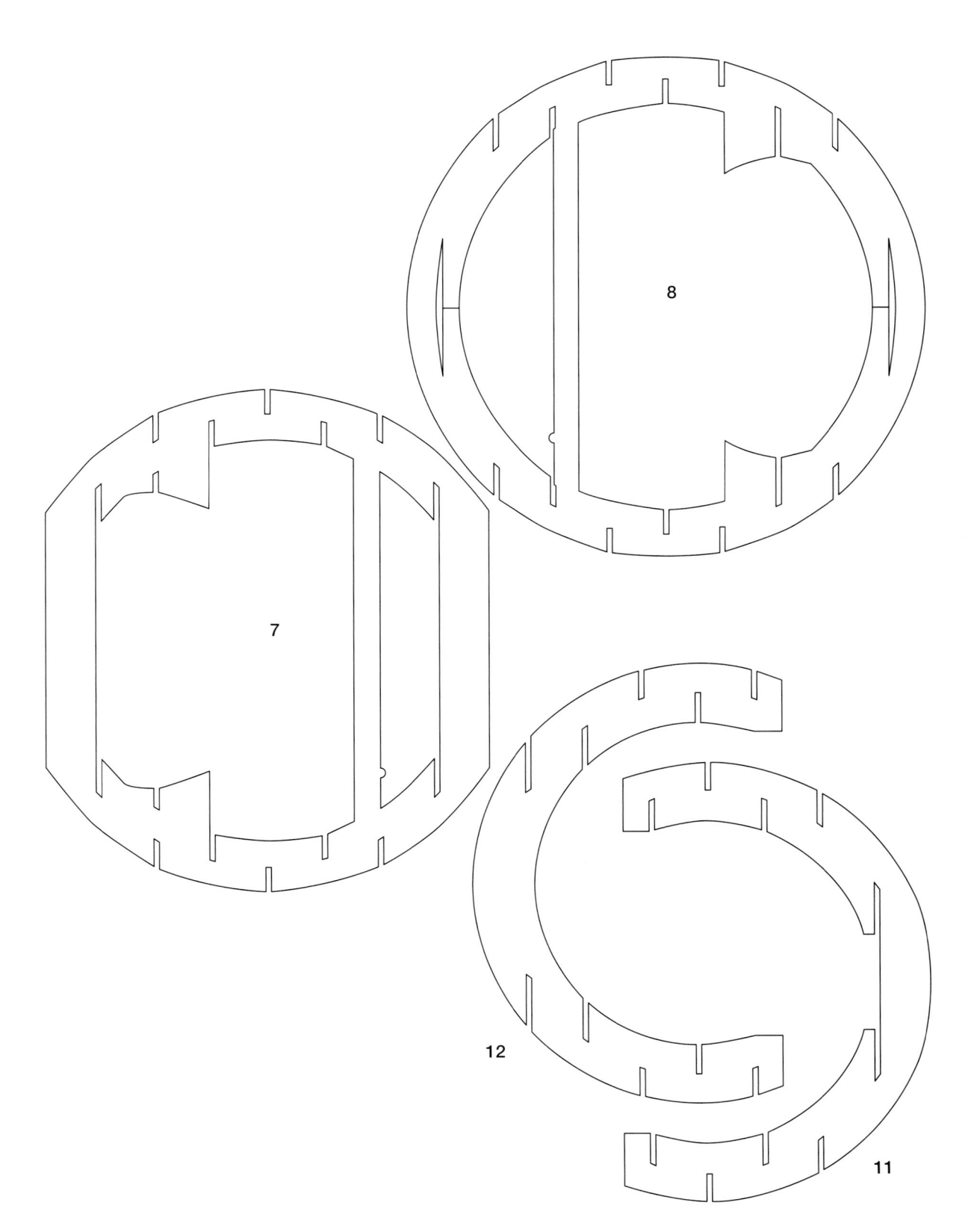

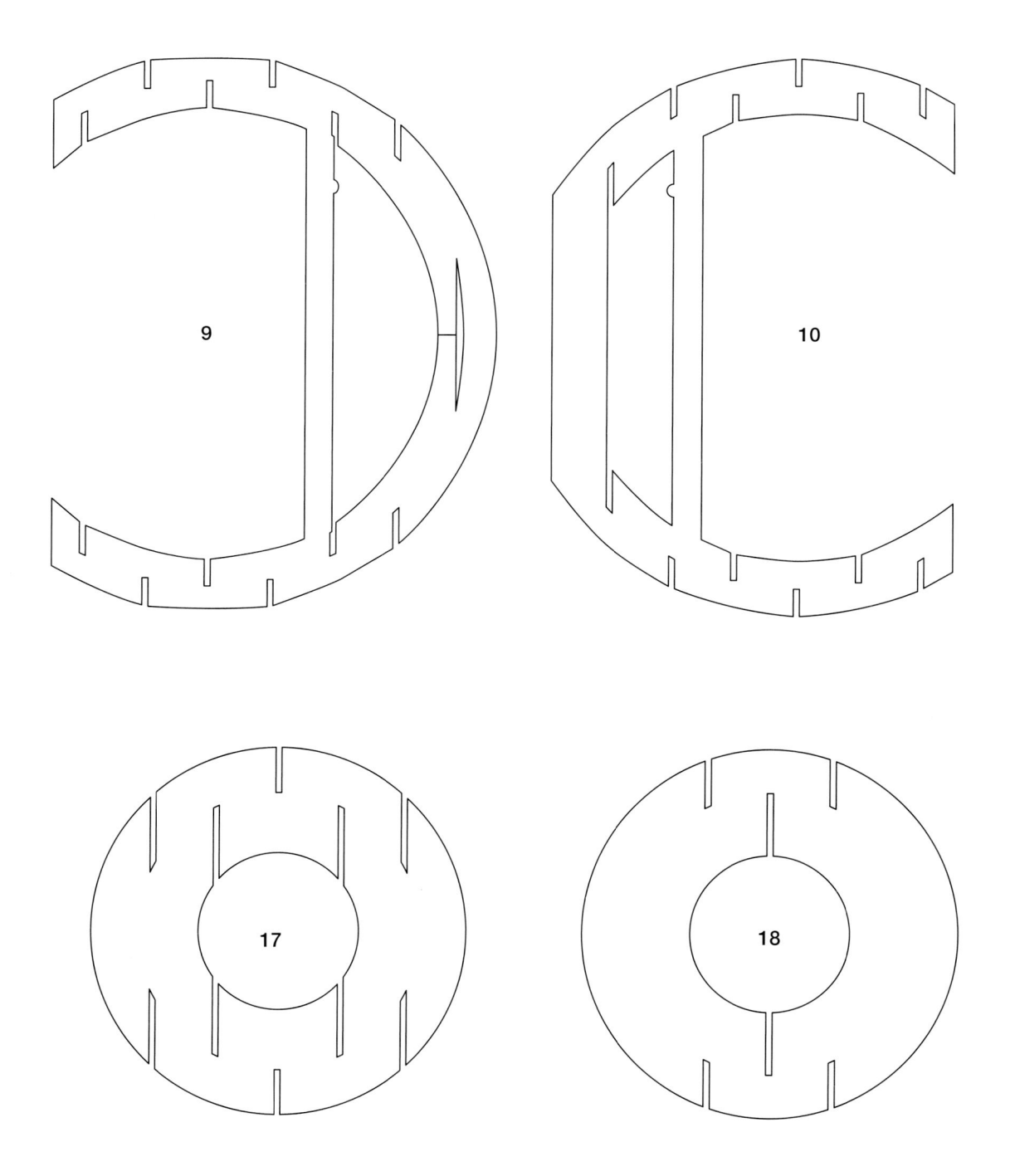

The center of a large sized card. Four rings have motifs.
See p. 52 for instructions.

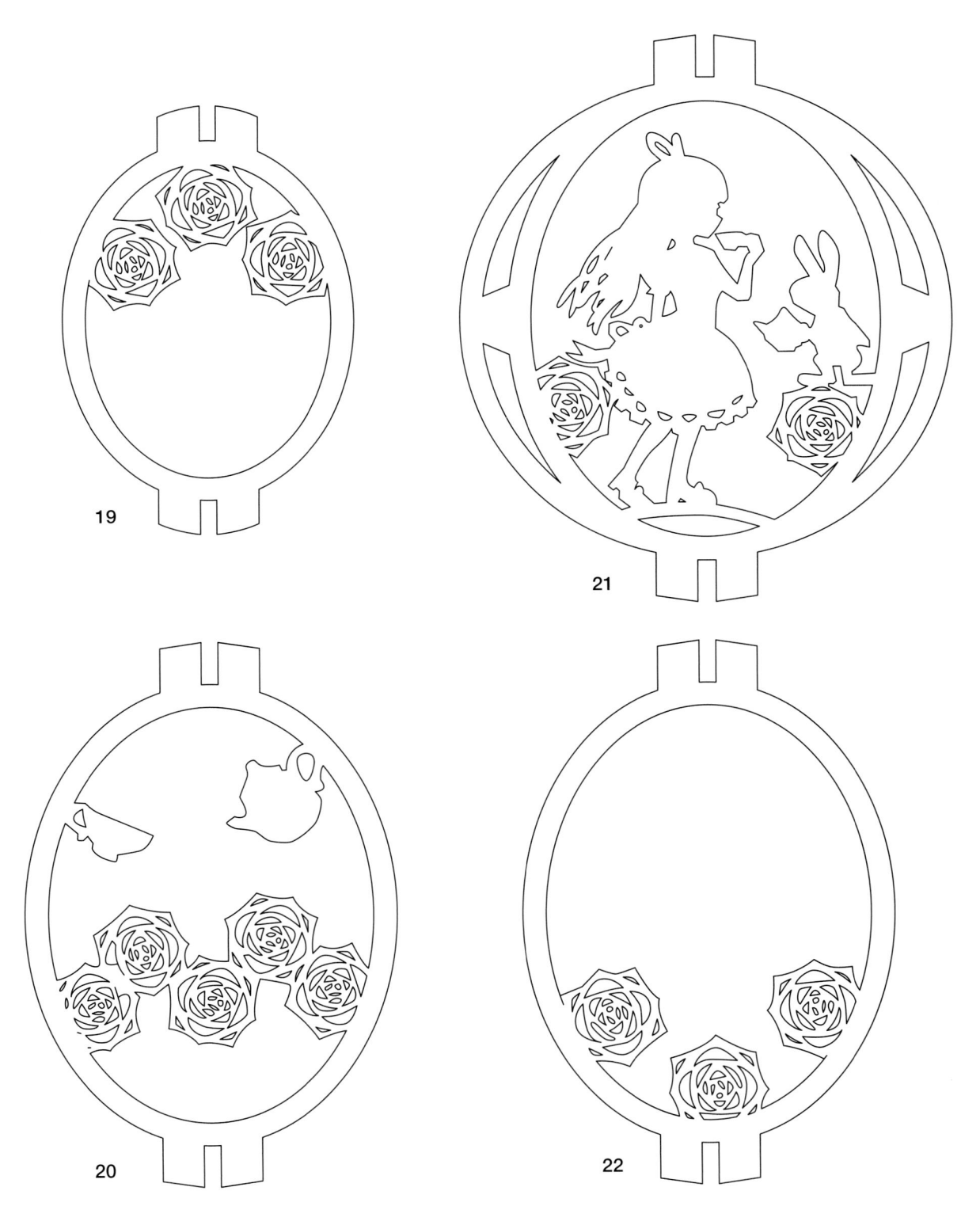

19

21

20

22

The center of a large sized card. Four rings have motifs.
See p. 52 for assembly instructions.

19

21

20

22

The center of a large sized card. Four rings have motifs.
See p. 52 for instructions.

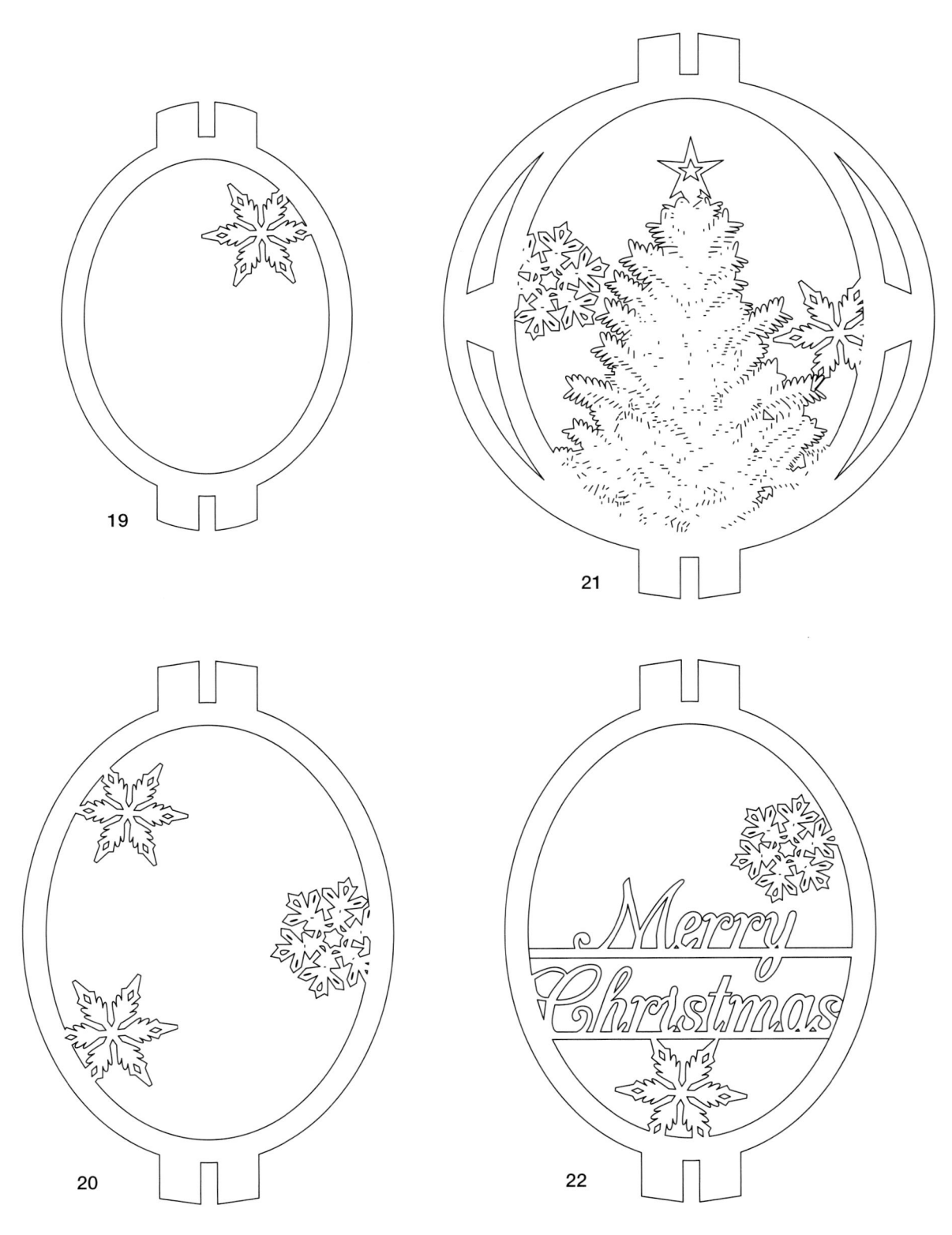

Paper artist **Seiji Tsukimoto** focuses on designing new paper ideas and enjoys translating themes of children's classic stories, fairy tales, and folklore, drawing from his native Japanese and from Western cultures. He continues to search for and create new types of pop-up designs. He lives in Chiba, Japan.

Other Schiffer Books on Related Subjects:

Papercutting: Geometric Designs Inspired by Nature, Patricia Moffett, ISBN 978-0-7643-5808-1

Folding Polyhedra: The Art & Geometry of Paper Folding, Alexander Heinz, ISBN 978-0-7643-6157-9

Paper Joy for Every Room: 15 Fun Projects to Add Decorating Charm to Your Home, Laure Farion, ISBN 978-0-7643-6055-8

English edition copyright © 2022 by Schiffer Publishing, Ltd.

Library of Congress Control Number: 2021953504

ISBN: 978-0-7643-6429-7

Printed in China

Published by Schiffer Publishing, Ltd.
4880 Lower Valley Road
Atglen, PA 19310
Phone: (610) 593-1777; Fax: (610) 593-2002
E-mail: Info@schifferbooks.com
Web: www.schifferbooks.com

For our complete selection of fine books on this and related subjects, please visit our website at www.schifferbooks.com. You may also write for a free catalog.

Schiffer Publishing's titles are available at special discounts for bulk purchases for sales promotions or premiums. Special editions, including personalized covers, corporate imprints, and excerpts, can be created in large quantities for special needs. For more information, contact the publisher.

We are always looking for people to write books on new and related subjects. If you have an idea for a book, please contact us at proposals@schifferbooks.com.

Japanese edition © 2016 Seiji Tsukimoto
Japanese edition © 2016 GRAPHIC-SHA PUBLISHING CO., LTD

First designed and published in Japan in 2016 by Graphic-sha Publishing Co., Ltd.
English edition published in the United States of America in 2022 by Schiffer Publishing, Ltd.

Original edition creative staff
Photos: Kazumasa Yamamoto
Art direction & layout: Satomi Nakata
Tracing: Kyodo Kogeisha
Editing: Ayako Enaka(Graphic-sha Publishing)

English edition creative staff
English translation: Kevin Wilson
English edition layout: Shinichi Ishioka
Foreign edition Production and management: Takako Motoki (Graphic-sha Publishing)

Cut out rings and use them to make the card.

See p. 18 for instructions.

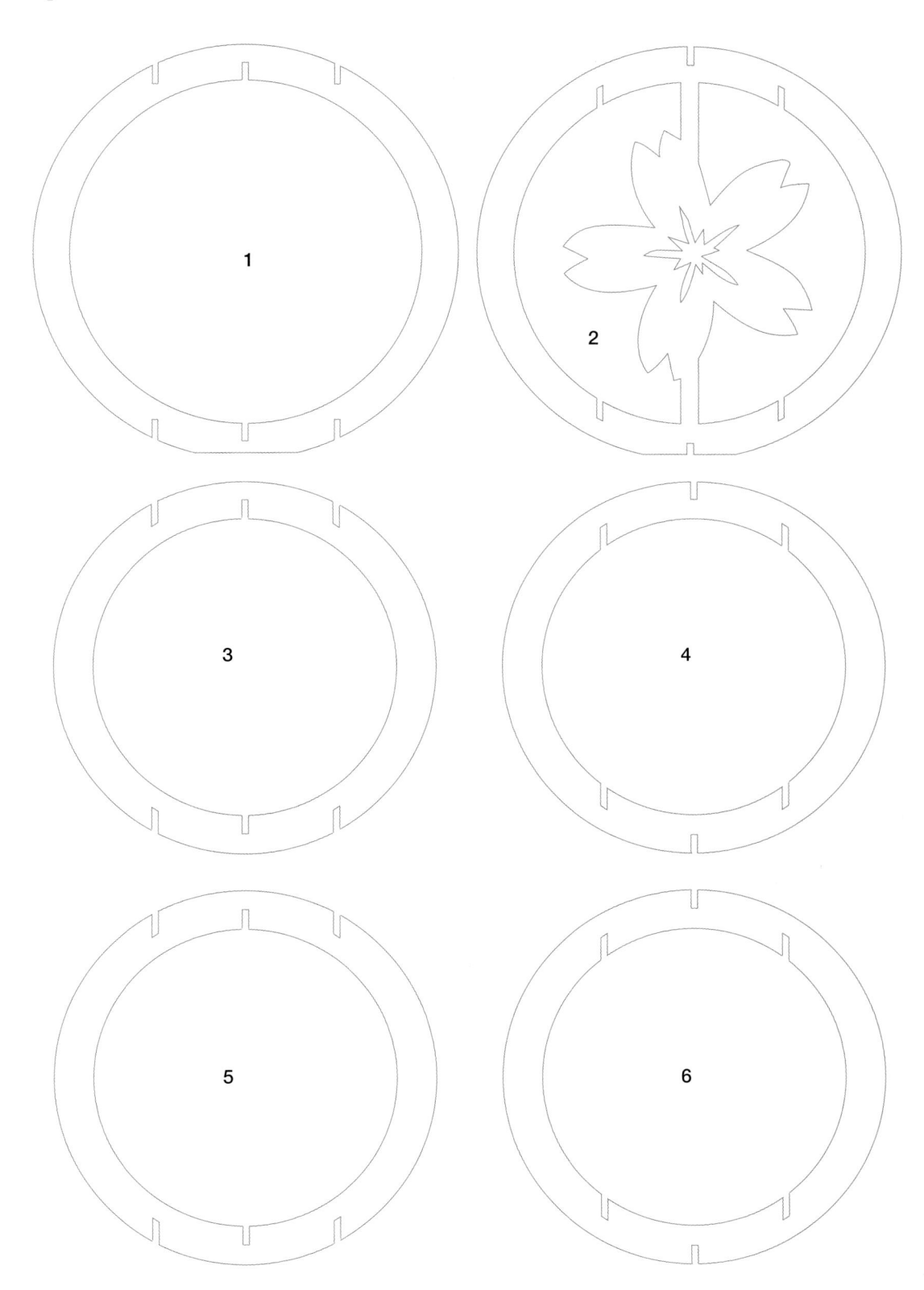

Cut Here

Cut out rings and use them to make the card.
See p. 18 for instructions.

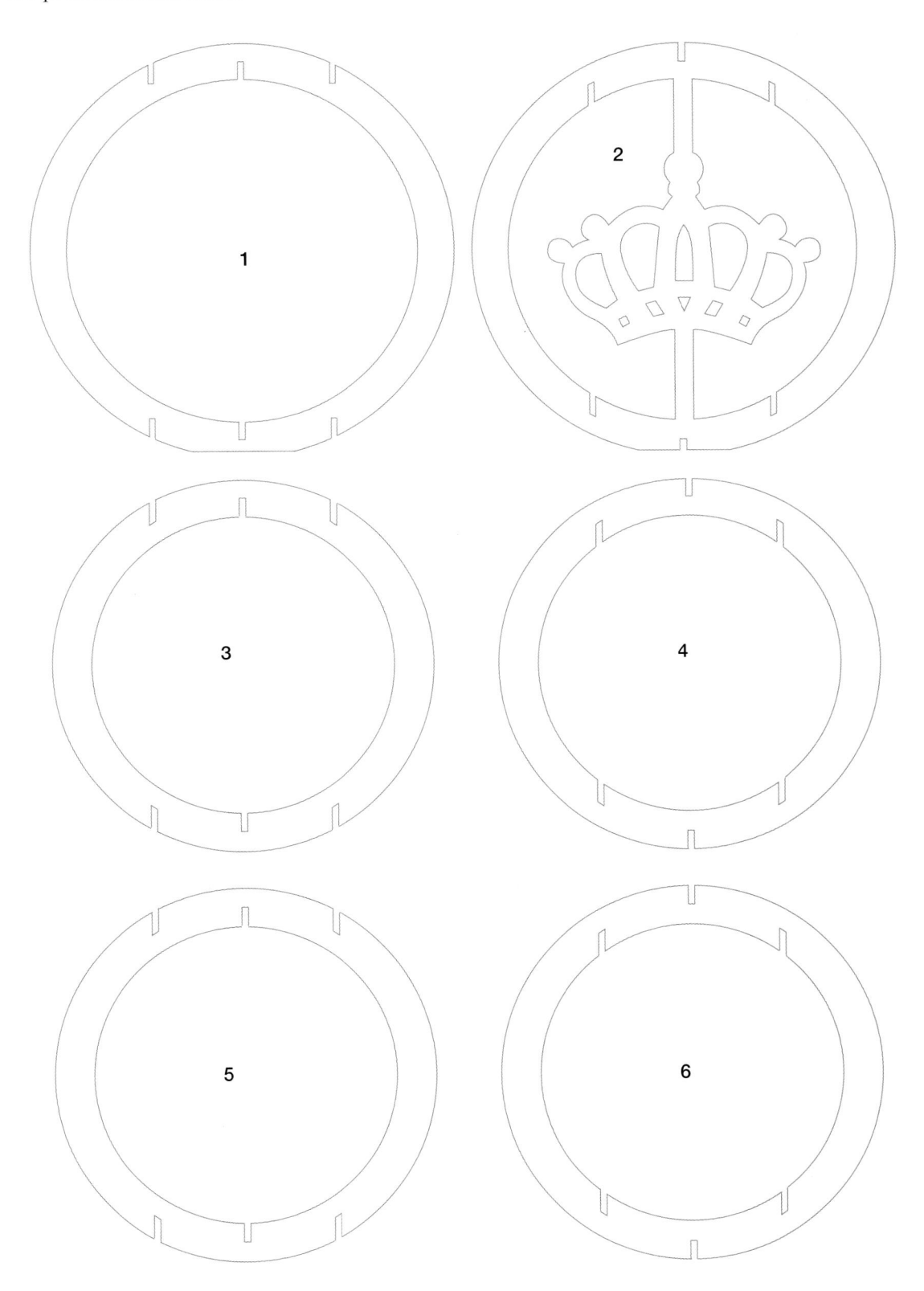

Cut Here

101

Cut Here

Detach p. 101 through p. 104. Cut out the rings and use them to make the card.
See p. 28 for instructions.

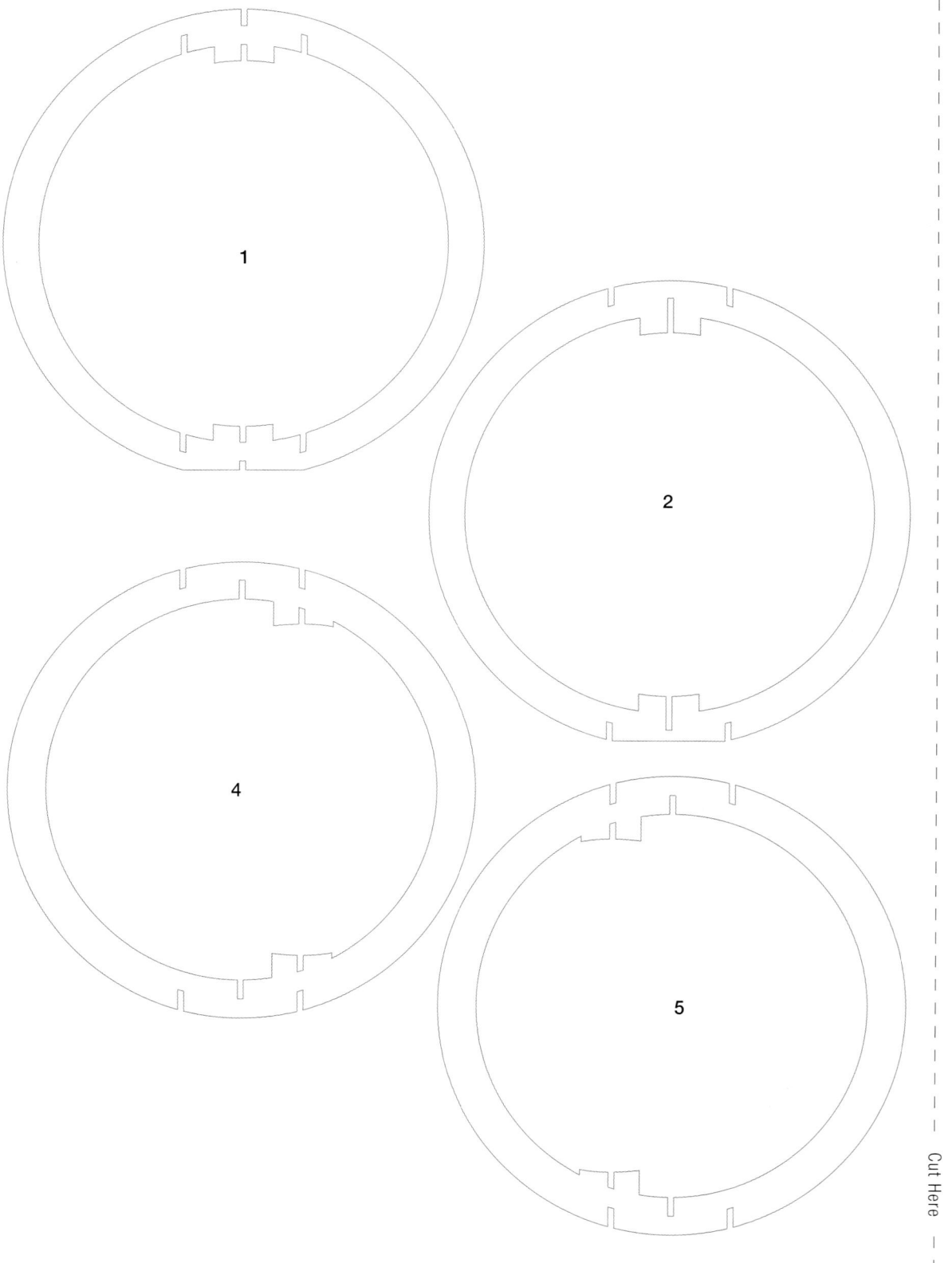

Cut Here

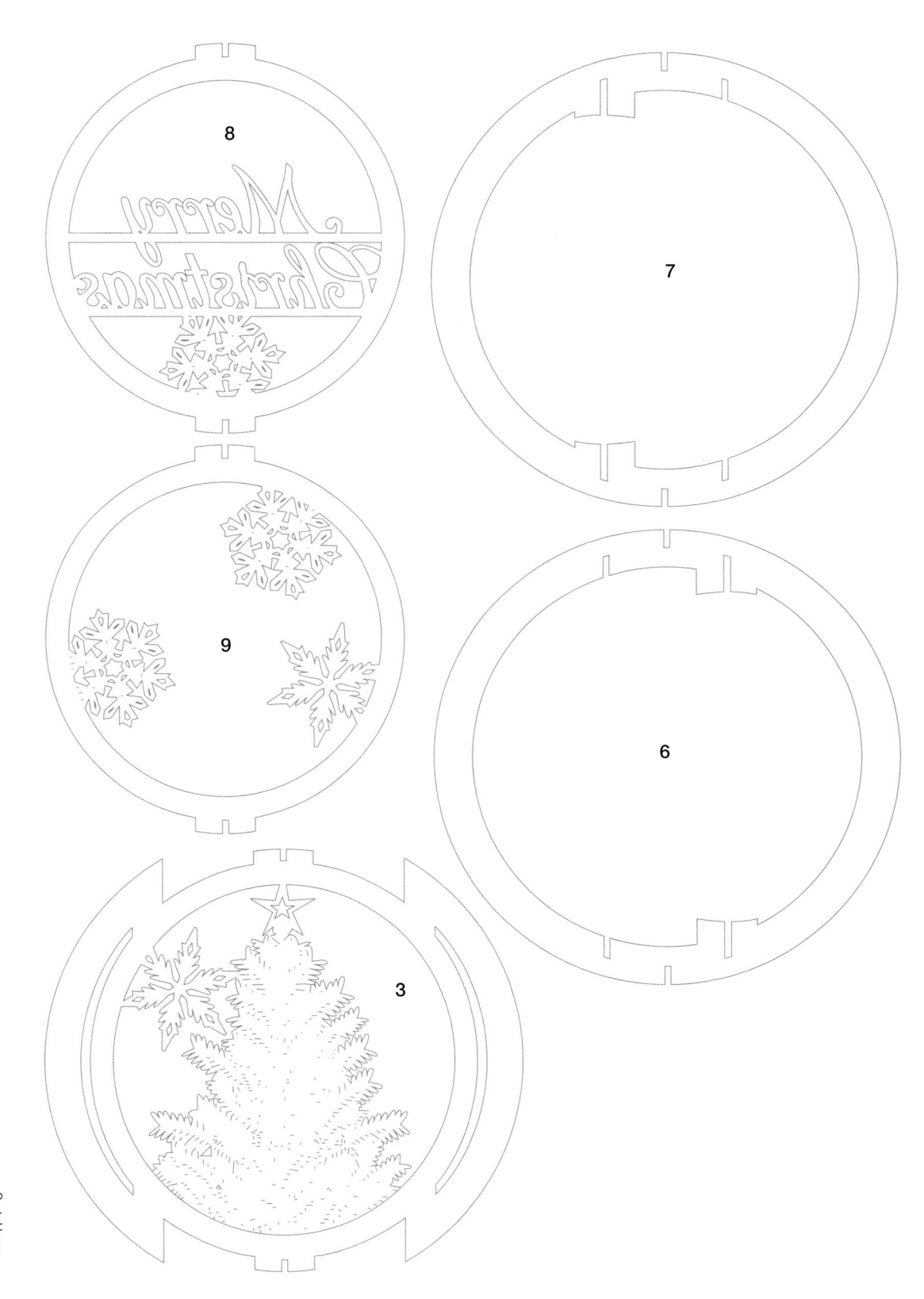

Cut Here

Detach p. 105 through p. 110. Cut out the rings and use them to make the card.
See p. 42 for instructions.

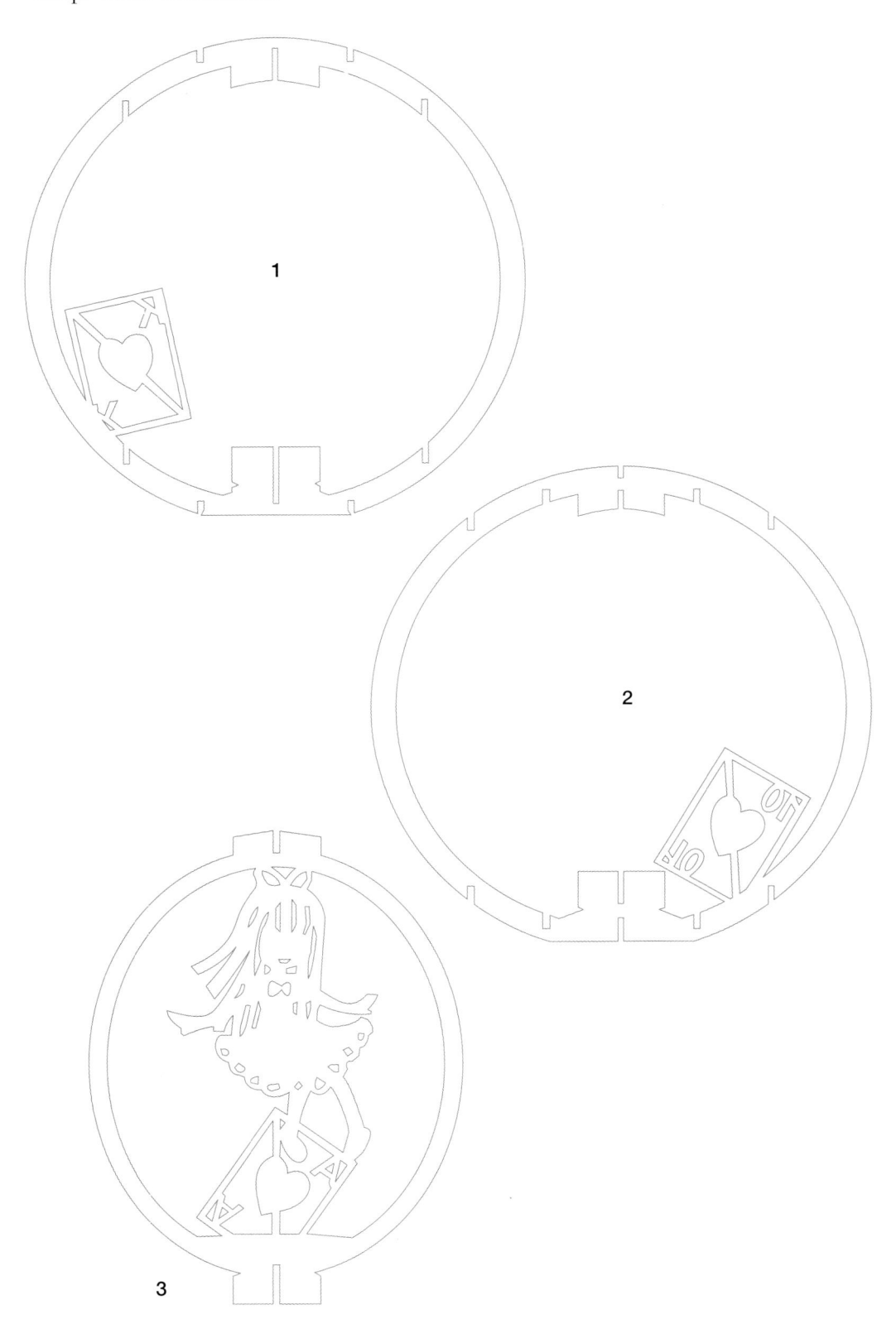

Cut Here

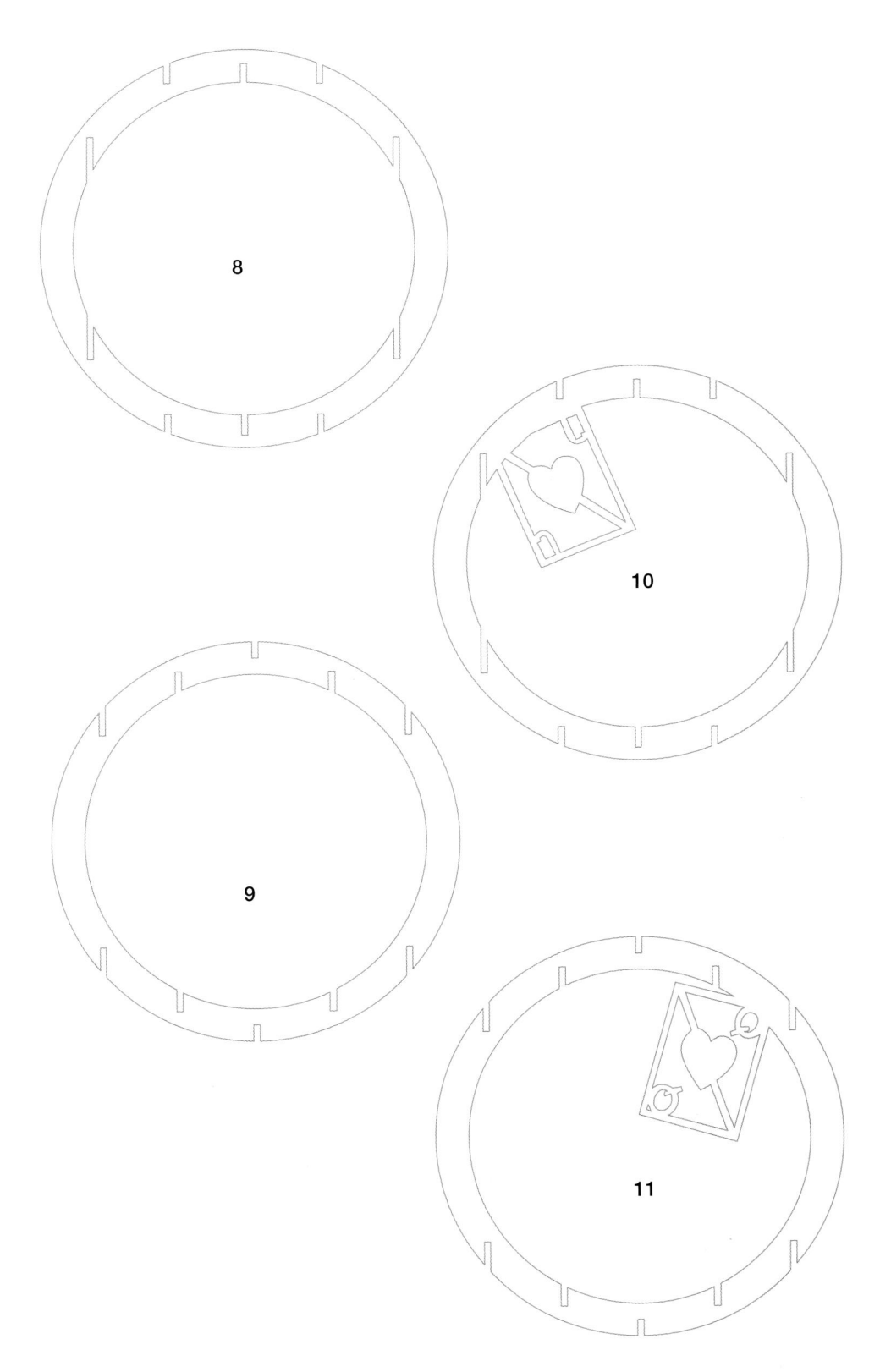

Cut Here

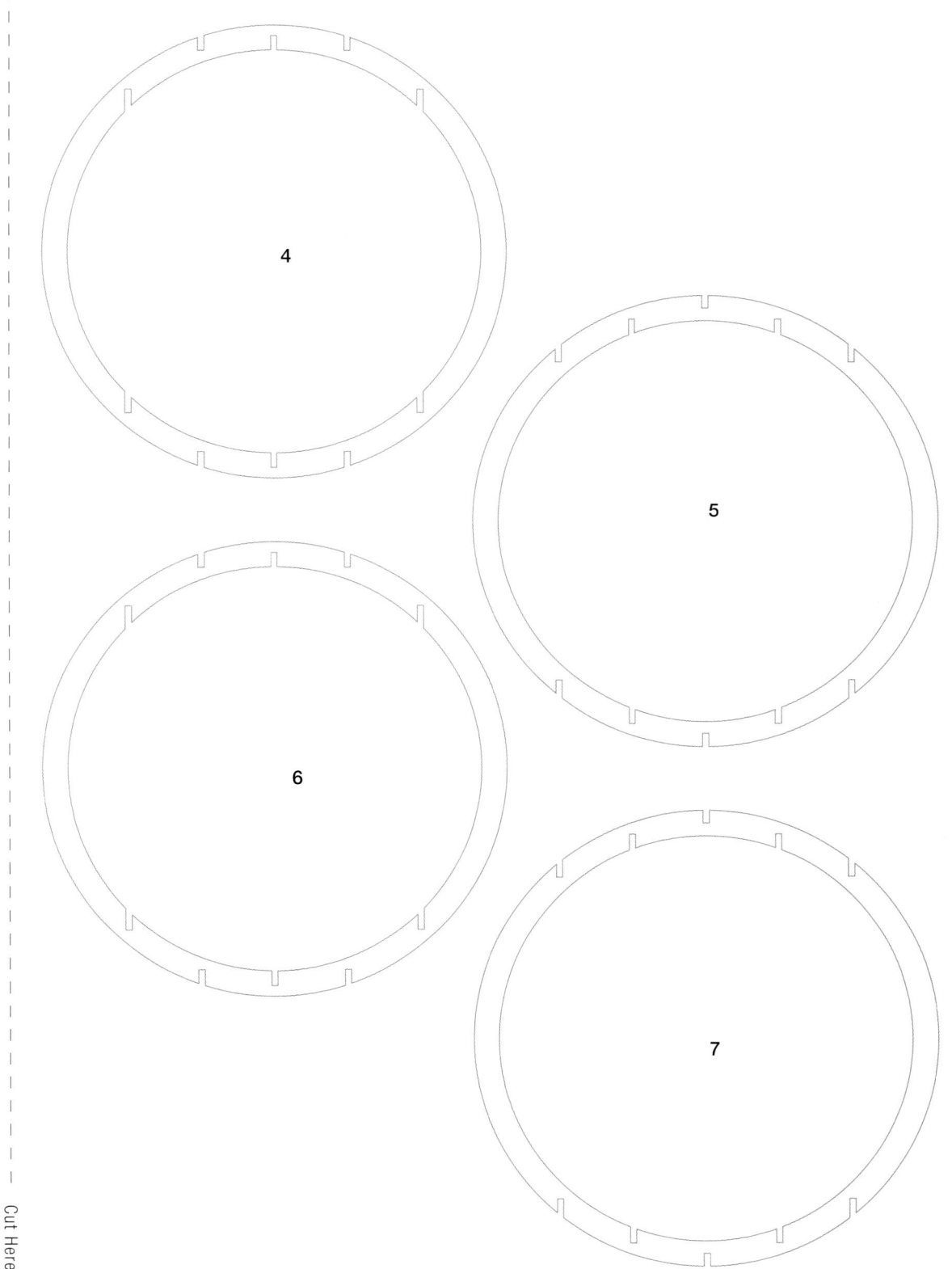

Cut Here

Cut Here

Detach p. 111 through p. 116. Cut out the rings and use them to make the card.
See p. 42 for instructions.

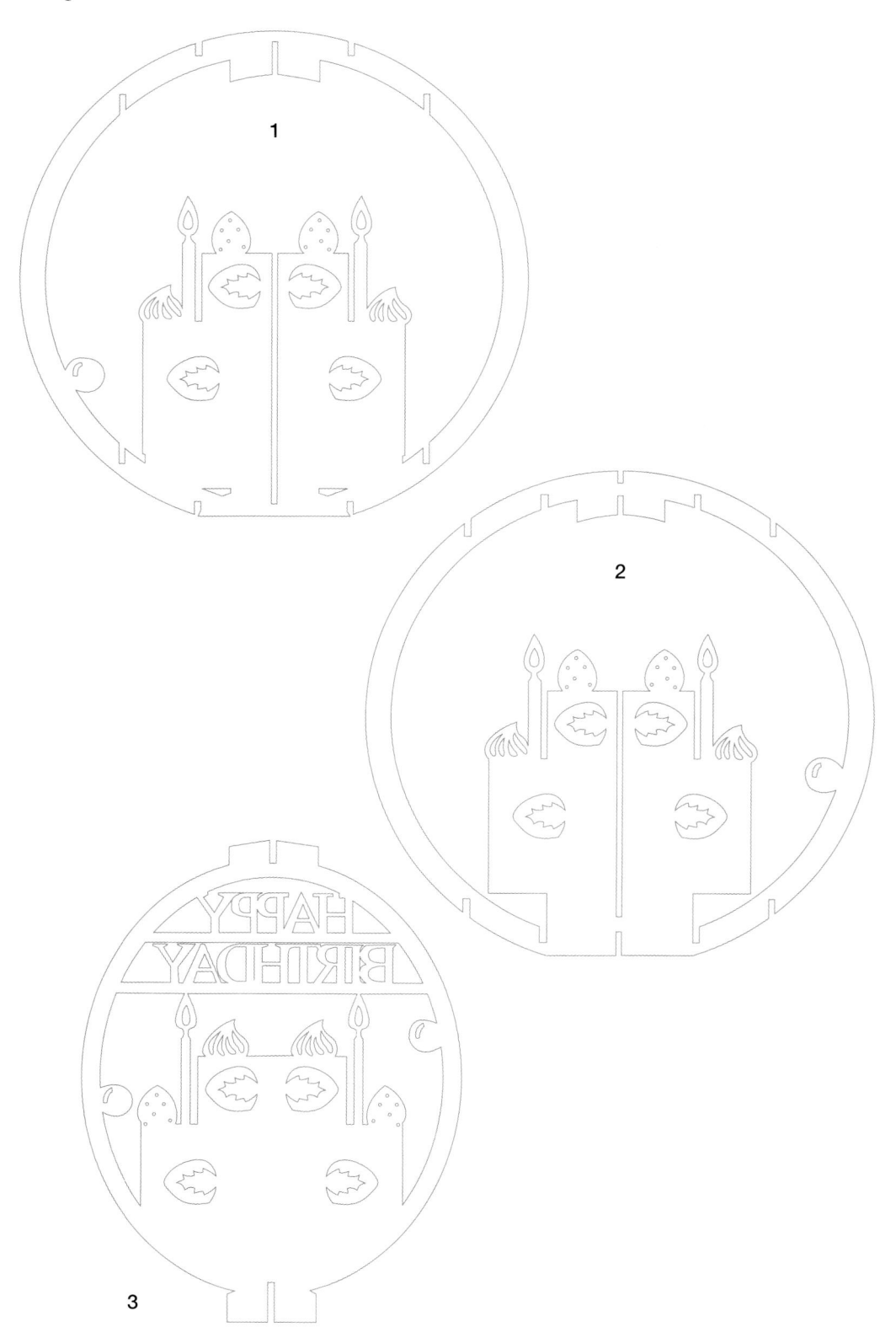

Cut Here

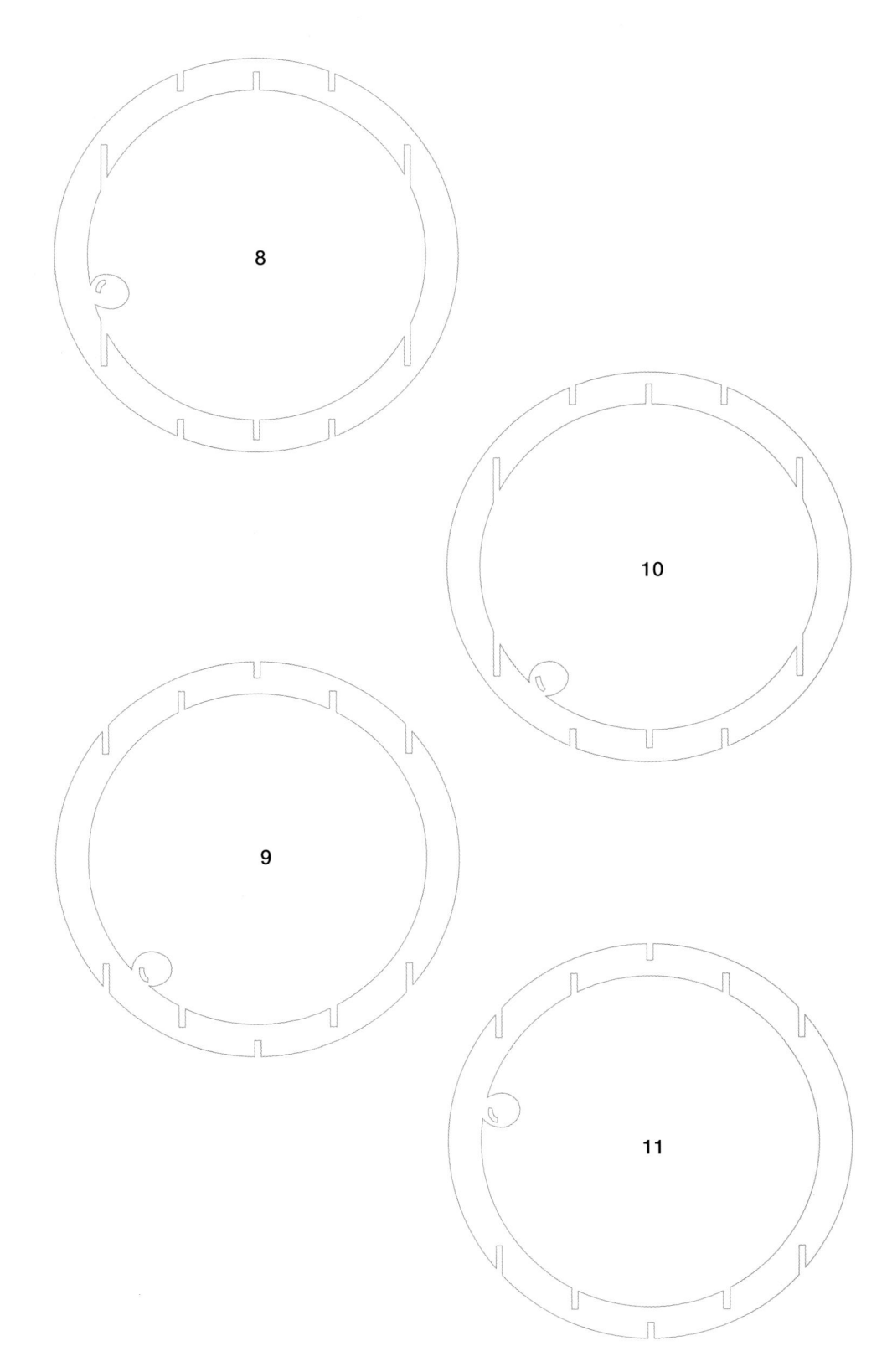

Cut Here

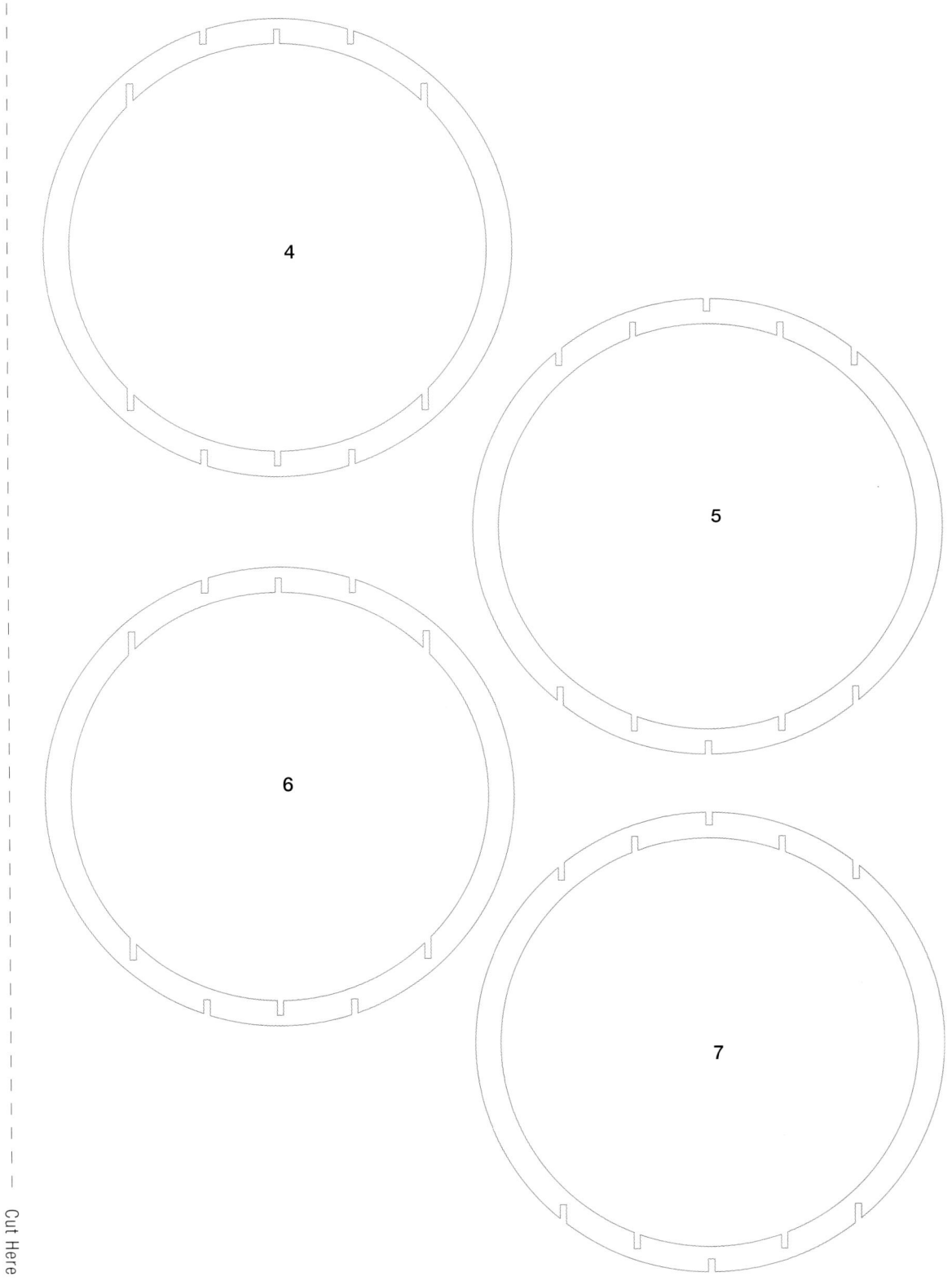

- Cut Here - - -

Detach p. 117 through p. 128. Cut out the rings and use them to make the card.
See p. 52 for instructions.

Cut Here

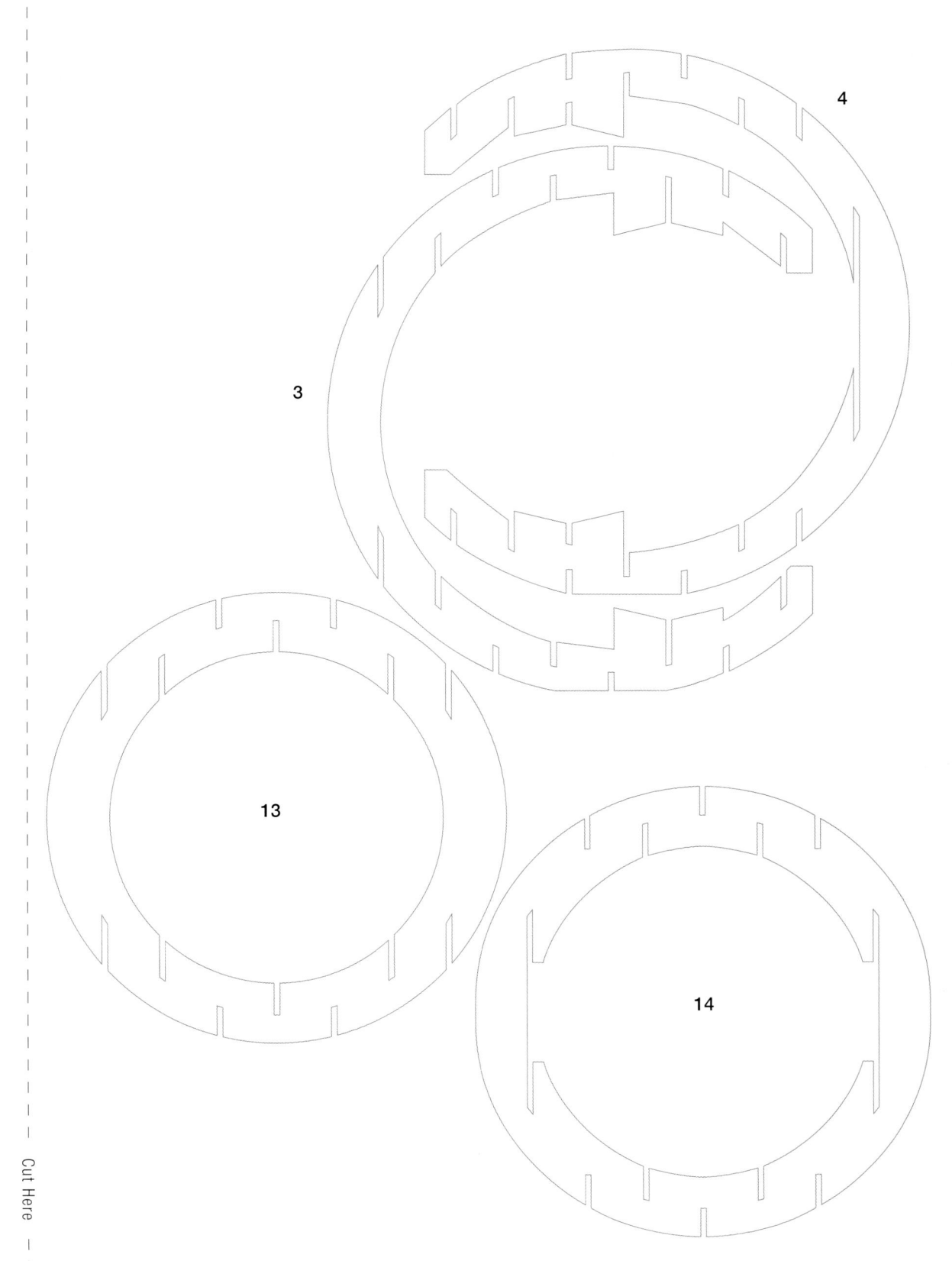

Cut Here

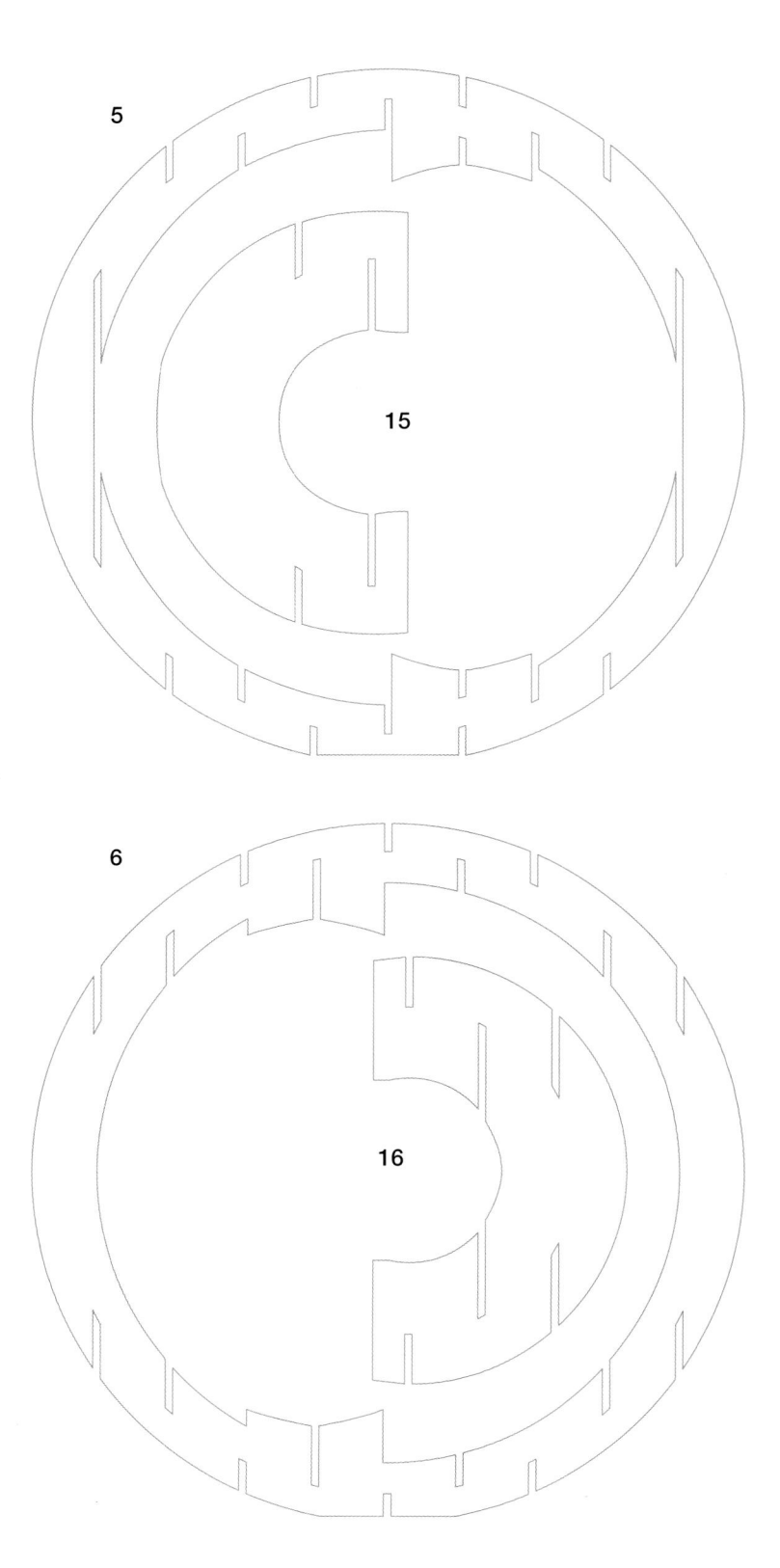

5

15

6

16

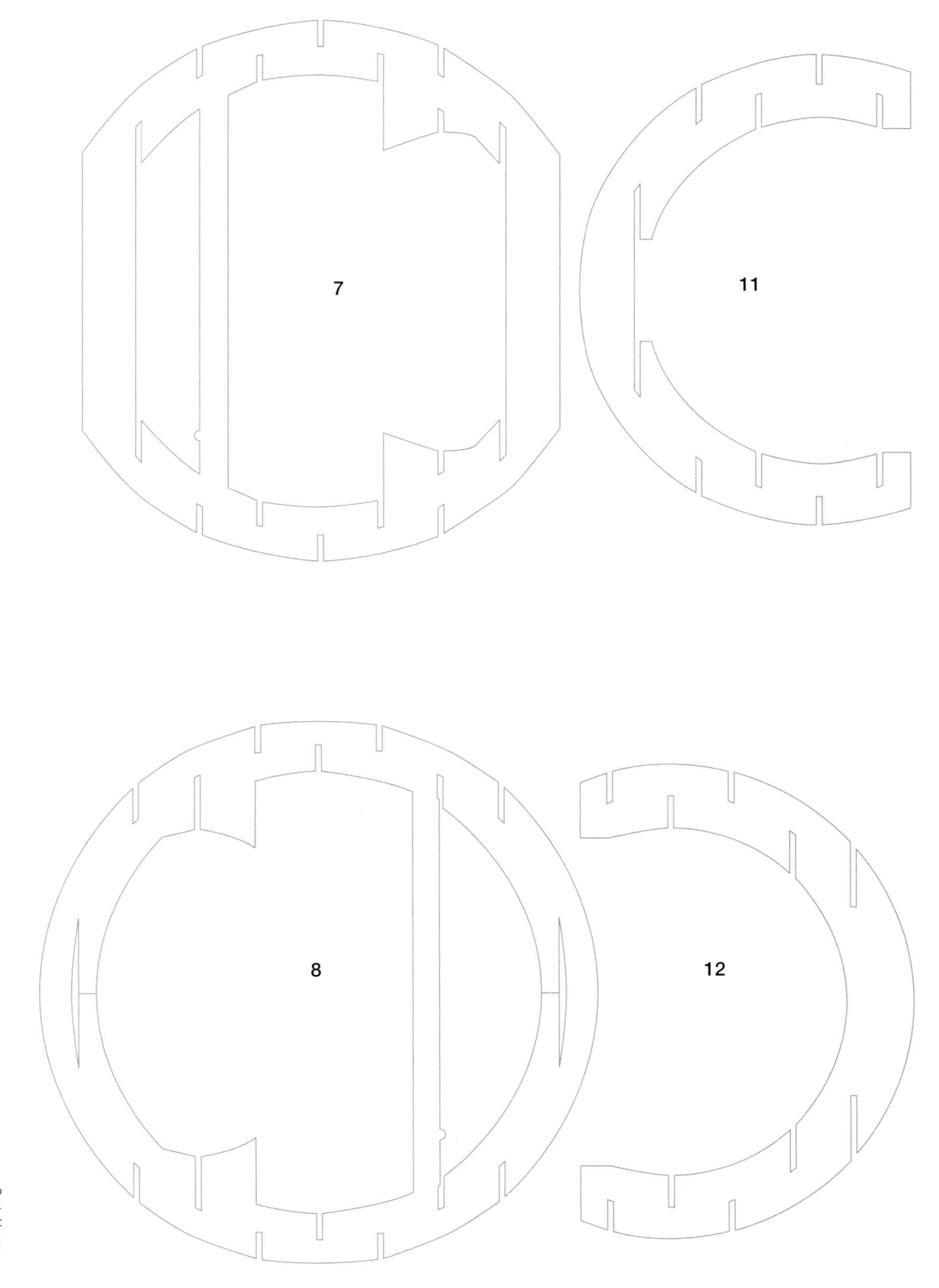

Cut Here

- Cut Here - - - - -

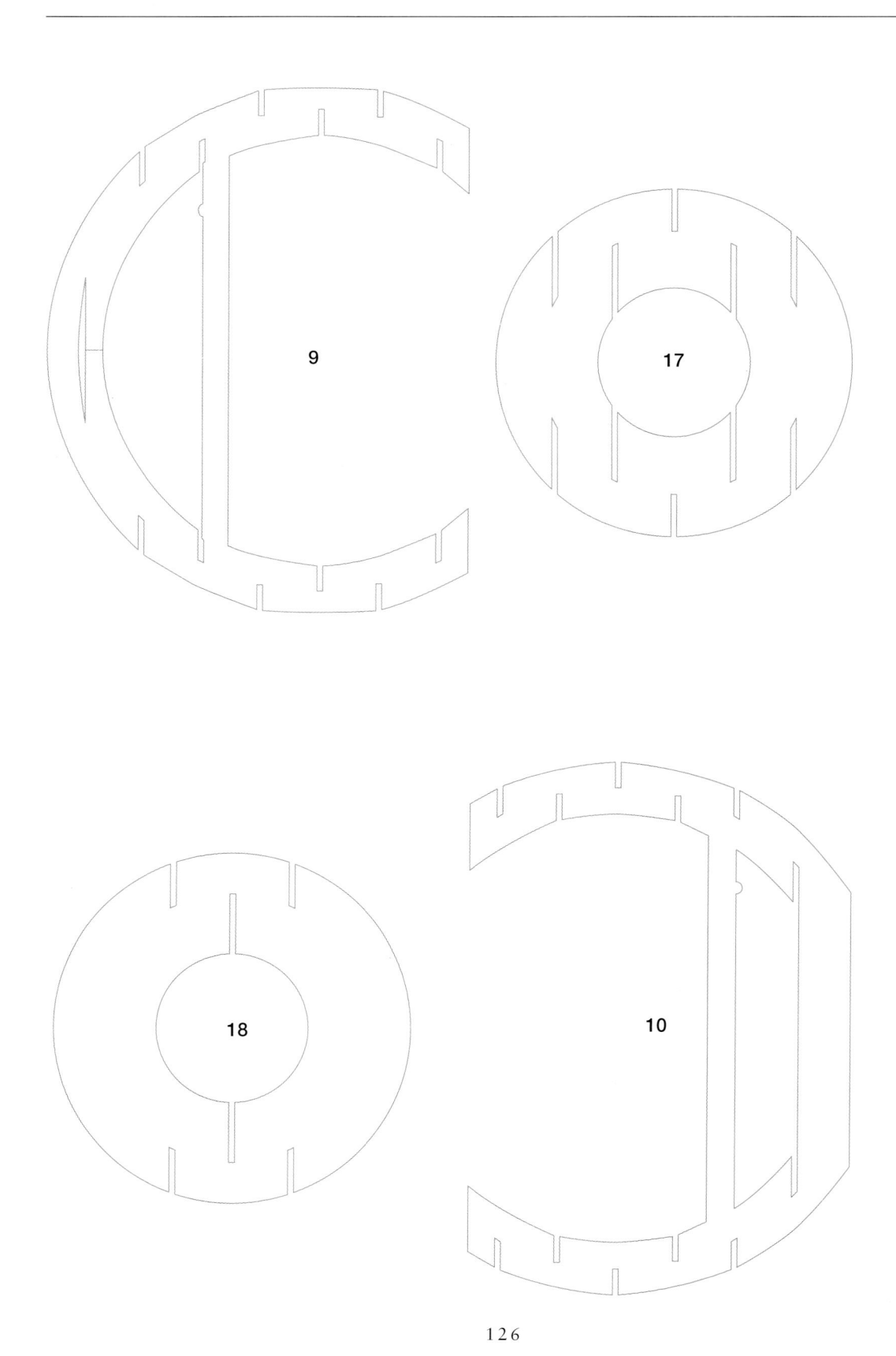

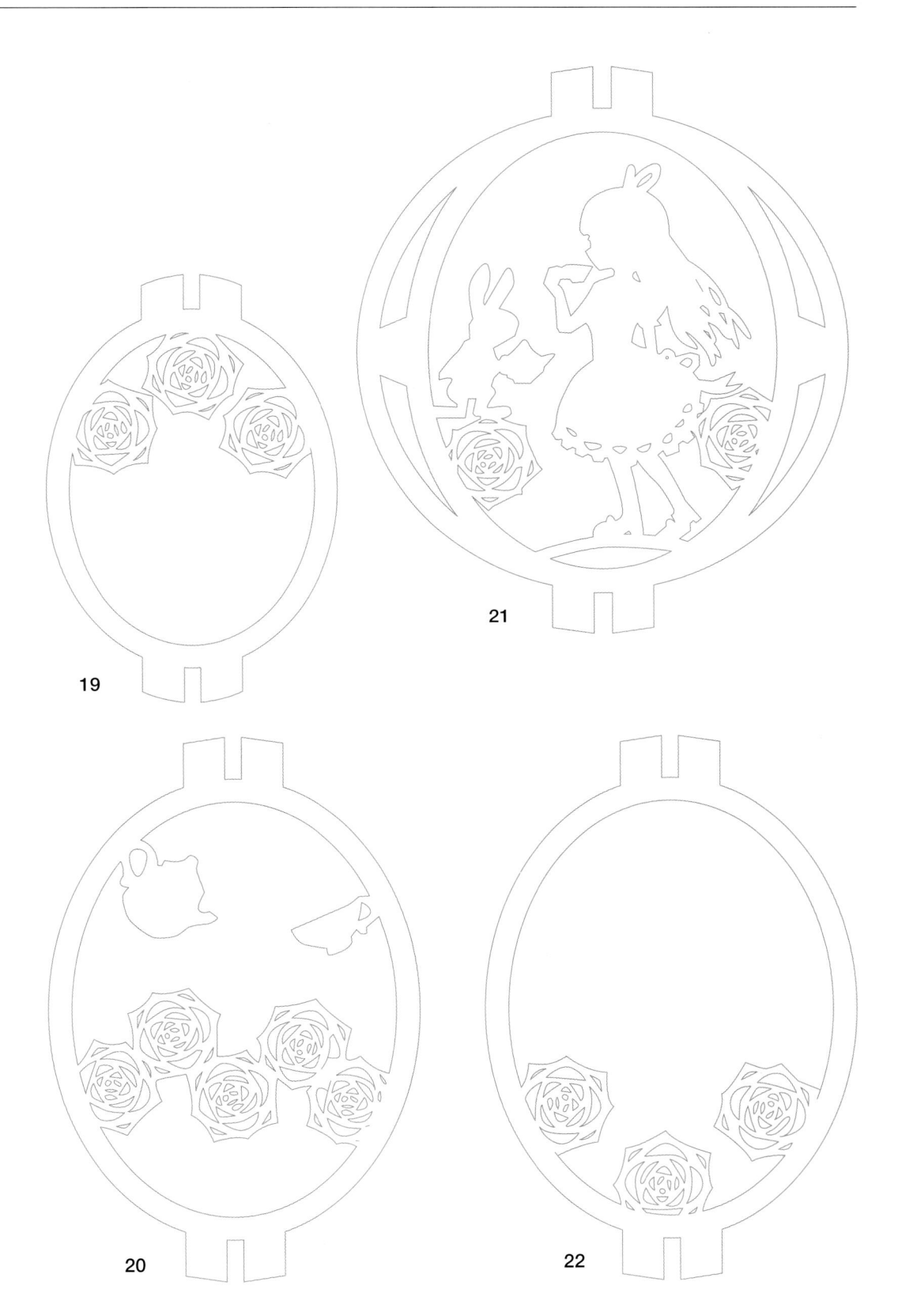

19

21

20

22

Cut Here